D0170679

Creating
The Good Will

APR 1 7 2002

Creating
The Good Will

THE MOST COMPREHENSIVE GUIDE TO BOTH THE FINANCIAL *AND* EMOTIONAL SIDES OF PASSING ON YOUR LEGACY

Elizabeth Arnold

PORTFOLIO

PORTFOLIO
Published by the Penguin Group
Penguin Group (USA) Inc., 375 Hudson Street, New York, New York 10014, U.S.A.
Penguin Group (Canada), 90 Eglinton Avenue East, Suite 700, Toronto, Ontario,
Canada M4P 2Y3 (a division of Pearson Penguin Canada Inc.)
Penguin Books Ltd, 80 Strand, London WC2R 0RL, England
Penguin Ireland, 25 St Stephen's Green, Dublin 2, Ireland
(a division of Penguin Books Ltd)
Penguin Books Australia Ltd, 250 Camberwell Road, Camberwell, Victoria 3124,
Australia (a division of Pearson Australia Group Pty Ltd)
Penguin Books India Pvt Ltd, 11 Community Centre, Panchsheel Park,
New Delhi – 110 017, India
Penguin Group (NZ), Cnr Airborne and Rosedale Roads, Albany, Auckland 1310,
New Zealand (a division of Pearson New Zealand Ltd)
Penguin Books (South Africa) (Pty) Ltd, 24 Sturdee Avenue, Rosebank,
Johannesburg 2196, South Africa

Penguin Books Ltd, Registered Offices: 80 Strand, London WC2R 0RL, England

First published in 2005 by Portfolio, a member of Penguin Group (USA) Inc.

1 3 5 7 9 10 8 6 4 2

Copyright © Elizabeth Arnold, 2005
All rights reserved

This publication contains the opinions and ideas of its author. It is intended to provide helpful and informative material on the subjects addressed in the publication. It is sold with the
understanding that the author and publisher are not engaged in rendering legal, accounting,
or any other kind of professional services in this book. The reader should consult a competent professional for legal, financial, or other professional advice before adopting any of the
suggestions in this book or drawing inferences from it. The author and publisher specifically
disclaim all responsibility for any liability, loss, or risk, personal or otherwise, which is incurred as a direct or indirect consequence of the use and application of any of the contents
of this book.
    The anecdotes in this book are drawn from real-life situations, but the names and other
identifying details have been changed.

LIBRARY OF CONGRESS CATALOGING-IN-PUBLICATION DATA
Arnold, Elizabeth, (Elizabeth A.)
Creating the good will / Elizabeth Arnold.
p.   cm.
Includes index.
ISBN 1-59184-119-4
1. Estate planning—United States—Popular works. 2. Estate planning—Psychological
aspects. I. Title.
KF750.Z9A76 2006
346.7305'2—dc22   2005053539

Printed in the United States of America
Designed by Nancy B. Field

Without limiting the rights under copyright reserved above, no part of this publication may
be reproduced, stored in or introduced into a retrieval system, or transmitted, in any form or
by any means (electronic, mechanical, photocopying, recording, or otherwise), without the
prior written permission of both the copyright owner and the above publisher of this book.

The scanning, uploading, and distribution of this book via the Internet or via any other
means without the permission of the publisher is illegal and punishable by law. Please purchase only authorized electronic editions and do not participate in or encourage electronic
piracy of copyrightable materials. Your support of the author's rights is appreciated.

*To everyone with the courage
to celebrate life and share who they are
with those they love.*

ACKNOWLEDGMENTS

I give heartfelt thanks to the following wonderful people:

To Jane Rohman and Molly Hamaker, without whose creativity, insights, and all-around brilliance this book and so much else would not have been possible. Words cannot begin to express the magnitude of my appreciation of and admiration for you and your many gifts. You are two phenomenal human beings. A big thanks to your families for generously sharing you to help with this project.

To my parents, Barbara and John Arnold, for lovingly walking their talk and giving us internal compasses to build our houses on stone—not to mention teaching us how to sing five-part harmony on really long station wagon trips. Pop, I wish you could be here: Nothing can bring me greater joy than remembering your roaring laughter. You may have left early, but you helped make us strong for what life might bring thereafter.

To my brother, John; my sister-in-law, Kara; and their three fabulous children: John, Kate, and Robert—and to my brother-in-law, Jan, and his children, the equally fabulous Sophie and Jahn-Otto, for your love and support. To my sister, Beverly, for her beautiful spirit that still lives on. I'll always miss you.

To my clients and friends, especially those who agreed to have their stories appear in this book (I hope you like your new names!), for inspiring me every day.

To Bernadette Malone, Will Weisser, Adrian Zackheim, and the rest of the fine crew at Penguin for your invaluable guidance and advice. From soup to nuts, working with you has been a delight—I hope we can do this again! Special thanks to Stephanie Land for believing in this book.

To my agent, Jim Levine, for sharing his sage counsel and wisdom.

To Ken Sweezey, my attorney, for helping to dot the i's and cross the t's on this project.

To Gail Heinzman and Rachael Maizes, who answered questions with grace and aplomb.

To Dawn Van Hee and John Bianco, for your excellent assistance on many fronts.

To Peggy Klaus, for your exuberant savvy, priceless input, all-around sense of fun, and the nickname Sprout.

To Evelyn Harris, Hans Frei, Wally Rohrbach, Dolliver Frederick, Amanda Kelly Courtemanche, Marc Hembrough, Susan Symons, Eleanor Criswell Hanna, Anna Maria and Brian Clement, Shannon Lee Turner, Mary Jarvis, Jane Boyer, Jesse Wilson, and Rachel Simon, whose belief in me has provided constant nourishment in this crazy, beautiful world.

CONTENTS

INTRODUCTION
Grief Gridlock

"Here one moment, gone the next."

It seems like just yesterday that Dad and I shared what was to become our last time together. On that beautiful autumn day in 1994, I was 28 and my 58-year-old father was seemingly healthy and in the prime of his life. It was my long-awaited first day working for my father after years of practicing law as an estate planning attorney.

That fateful day, Dad had spent the morning walking me around the office and introducing me to the employees. Everyone chuckled when he lightheartedly remarked, "This is Elizabeth; she'll be here long after I'm gone." Later at lunch, we conversed about love, life, business, and his estate. Dad's eyes welled up with tears as he asked me to forgive him for not getting me involved sooner in the business. I took his hand and told him that we had plenty of time left but gently chided him for putting off some pressing issues in his estate plan.

The following morning as I prepared for my second day on the job, starting out with a brisk sprint on the Nordic track, the phone rang. It was Mom. Dad had taken a fall that morning. She had awakened to the love of her life collapsing down the stairs as he got up for a glass of milk. She said, "Don't worry, but get to the hospital immediately."

Ever the optimist, entering the emergency room I imagined seeing my father sitting up, sporting a neck brace, and making light of his clumsiness. As I was quickly escorted into a private area, however, I was met with a completely different image. There he was, his body stretched out on a gurney with his beloved curly silver mop on one end and skinny long legs sticking out of an all-too-short hospital gown on the other. As I stepped closer to look into his loving face, I realized his once twinkling blue eyes were completely vacant.

And just like that, in a heartbeat, Pop was gone.

What My Dad Really Wanted: Despite His Will, No One Agreed

Dad and Mom had kept their estate plan in tip-top shape for years. It was a model in tax planning structures. Their plan for the three offspring was to give a third to each child, a simple enough formula on paper but with enough fluid parts and communication blind spots to blow the family apart. I knew what Dad had told me he envisioned the day before he died, but my siblings, in-laws, and mother held onto their own recollections of scattered conversations throughout the years. Although I had a written agreement regarding my new position in the company, family members began to challenge it within hours of my father's passing. And within days, someone was even questioning my share of the inheritance, wondering if something should be deducted for the expense that went into funding my Ivy League education—despite that our parents would have provided that opportunity for them had they chosen the same path. I couldn't believe what I was hearing. But this wasn't my family talking. It was grief gridlock.

Equally striking was that nothing in the estate plan fully encapsulated my father's legacy—absent was any mention of his hopes and dreams for us and his values. Unquestionably, having these thoughts explicitly expressed would have helped us more quickly step beyond the bricks and mortar, beyond the tangibles, and beyond the money.

While on the outside our family was the model of good behavior, behind closed doors tensions began escalating that would take years to resolve. The lid was off Pandora's box. My father's will had become a lightning rod for our anguish, grief, frustrations, anger, and confusion—a gateway for unfilled emotional needs and unresolved hurts among family members. If my father had witnessed this scene on earth, he would have certainly been deeply disappointed in all of us.

During this difficult period, I found myself returning to two predominate "if only . . ." thoughts.

If only my dad had lived long enough to create the unambiguous, loving, and lasting communication he had intended—all of this conflict could have been avoided and our family could have completely focused on celebrating his life and legacy.

If only I had seen this coming.

But, in fact, I had.

Beyond the Stuff: What Harvard Left Out of the Textbooks

Long before my dad died, I used to drive my law professors nuts asking about what happened inside families when tax-driven estate plans became actualized in real life. Growing up, I had seen too many horror stories among my parents' friends whose estate plans in action wreaked havoc due to inadequate consideration of the human component when creating them. How many people do you know in your own family and others who don't share Thanksgiving together, or who don't talk to each other because so-and-so got X from a will?

In the early 1990s, Harvard Law wouldn't touch the emotional side of estate planning with a ten-foot pole. Not only are these human issues impossible to quantify, but every situation is different. Helping people navigate this tricky turf requires a completely different skill-set than what law school graduates are typically trained to produce: clear, watertight legal structures that protect assets and transition them to loved ones. Even now, most textbooks and consumer guides on creating wills skim over the human side of estate planning.

While working as an estate attorney and representing feuding families, my experience yet again confirmed how even the best legal structures could destroy families when the human elements weren't simultaneously addressed. I spent days in a courtroom hearing mothers and sons rip each other to shreds rather than talk to each other about the real issues. I spent hours in my office helping clients resolve disputes over who would get the deceased's beloved collection of birdhouses while a multimillion-dollar business hung in the balance. As a result, I often put in extra time off the clock with clients and family friends, helping them acquire essential skills and implement strategies that would protect their families in the future from, well, themselves.

Although I had tried my best to forewarn my father of these estate time bombs for years, he kept putting off addressing these emotional issues for a variety of reasons from "not enough time" to "waiting for the kids' lives to settle down." Despite my warnings, I felt disempowered to do anything about it because it wasn't my estate. Worse-case scenario, if something bad did happen, I hoped that our strongly shared values would pull my family through—which, despite years of preventable in-fighting after my father's death, eventually happened. After all, my parents had raised us as a cohesive and loving unit. Family came first before anything else. We were never treated as children of privilege. We went to public schools, lived in a modest home, worked summer jobs, and were expected to get good grades. My father often reminded us that our family business had succeeded from one generation to the next through nothing more than pure sweat and good luck. And it could all be gone tomorrow.

But most of all, I thought time was on our side. Don't we all? As it turned out, it wasn't.

New Beginnings: Sowing Seeds

While my family endured some tough times after my father's death, we eventually made our way to a better place. The tragedy is that our wounds and scars could have been avoided. The blessing is that we were able to achieve family peace in time before my sister tragically died in a small plane crash in Norway in the spring of 2003.

Before long, after leaving the family business, people started to call on me again for estate planning advice. I tinkered with the idea of getting back into law full time, but was drawn instead to another calling: saving families both grief and money by helping them to address the emotional dimension often overlooked in well-intentioned, but misguided, estate plans and last wills prepared by $300-an-hour attorneys. Once I started advising folks again, I found myself quietly focusing on communication blind spots—the perceptions and expectations that can make or break the most ironclad legal documents. And before I knew it, I was showing them how to use the estate planning process to build bridges with loved ones and celebrate their lives.

People quickly embraced my new approach, which I later came to call The Good Will. One that puts the emotional well-being of families ahead of clever tax-saving structures. One that celebrates lives more than hard assets. One that strengthens family relationships as much in the *here and now* as in the hereafter. One that addresses the complicated family structures that are so common in our modern times. One that breathes fresh air into the daunting, technical process of estate planning—turning it ultimately from a dreaded affair into a surprisingly freeing and fulfilling one.

The Good Will is not just created in an attorney's office. It's not just created by making sure you've dotted the i's and crossed the t's on legal forms. It's not just created by jumping through tax loopholes. While no doubt these things are important, creating the Good Will is ultimately about people and what matters most to you and your loved ones.

I often tell others that I started my present company, Sowing Seeds, in a hospital room in Harrisburg on an autumn morning in 1994. My life's work found me at that moment and influenced me ever since to help others sow the seeds of their legacy by using the estate planning process to celebrate life and create family harmony, not havoc. My legacy has become helping others create theirs.

Looking back now it seems fortuitous that after my father's death, one of my most cherished mementos became a card that he had handed me on my 18th birthday in which he had simply scribbled, *"It's up to you kid. Pass it on."*

And so with this book—which encapsulates the tools and strategies I have developed and used to help thousands of individuals and families find greater joy and peace—I now pass it on to you, with the hope that you will in turn pass it on to those you love.

Elizabeth Arnold

Creating The Good Will

"What do you do?" asked Denise, the petite 50-something brunette seated next to me during breakfast at a Washington, D.C., hotel. We had just met and were both in town for an estate planning seminar—she as an attendee and I as the morning's speaker. Whenever I tell people that I am a crisis-prevention coach for families dealing with estate plans, they unleash frustration about the dilemmas they've faced when developing their own plans or tell me about family discord resulting from a misguided, inadequate, or altogether nonexistent will. Everyone has a story. I bet you are thinking of your own right now. Stories of how Aunt Sue nabbed the vase and how Aunt Pat hasn't spoken a kind word to her since. Stories of irreparably hurt feelings from colliding expectations in families who once hung tightly together. Stories about the thorny issues surrounding who gets the kids and who gets what. Stories about loved ones tap-dancing around the difficult subject of death. Throughout the years, I've been told thousands of these stories, running the gamut from families with modest means to those owning billion-dollar hotel chains. In fact, in just one day last week, I heard three—beginning with my breakfast-mate Denise's tale, a true case of whodunit.

A FAMILY HEIRLOOM RAISES HAIRS

Apparently, Denise's great-great-grandmother was a superb writer who had painstakingly recorded in diaries her secret and dangerous work with the Underground Railroad during the Civil War. These stories had become the stuff of family lore and legend. Denise and her ten cousins were raised keenly aware of the sacrifices and bravery of this pioneering woman. The diaries, however, which Denise tells me in whispers are worth a slight fortune today, had mysteriously disappeared from the attic of her grandmother who had recently passed away. The grandmother had assumed the volumes would be handed down to the next generation, no questions asked, and hadn't bothered to mention them in her will. Everyone had theories about which family member was last seen cleaning out the attic, but no one would fess up. Family gatherings, which for generations had been much-cherished events, were now shrouded with whispers, insinuations, and outright hostility. Uncle Kevin was pointing fingers at Aunt Lucy. Aunt Lucy was pointing fingers at Uncle Barry. Uncle Barry was resting the blame at Aunt Vanessa's feet. Now, all the cousins were barely on speaking terms. It was like a game of Clue with no end in sight.

HOUSEGATE: A CHERISHED FAMILY HOME

By mid-morning, Diarygate had been replaced with Housegate. While taking up the conference sponsor's offer of a complimentary massage at the hotel spa, the masseuse asked me what I did for a living. Half asleep and caught off guard, I told him. The gentle massage, which only moments ago was lulling me into a deep state of relaxation, now became a sharp poke and a hard press as Mr. Masseuse related the story of a vacation home that had been in his family for nearly twenty years. His mother and father had always said, "Don't worry, the house will go to you children when we die." But his mother had died sooner than any of them would have imagined, and their father had remarried an older woman named Betty with five adult children of her own. When his father died last fall, after being married to Betty for seven years, he had left the vacation home to his new wife in the will.

Before his death, when Mr. Masseuse and his siblings had tried to broach the touchy subject of their desire to keep the house for the original family, his father scoffed at their fears and repeatedly said, "Don't worry, you won't get cheated. I trust Betty completely. Plus, she lives closer to the place than any of you do and will be able to take good care of it for the whole family." Now, Mr. Masseuse wasn't so sure. Having just returned from a two-week vacation at the property, he could see his cherished, memory-filled home slipping away. For starters, although Betty had assured him that those two weeks were available for his exclusive use, within two days of arrival, his stepsister—whom he hardly knew—showed up for a long weekend with her screaming toddler twins in tow. "Some vacation!" he huffed, adding, "What's worse, my father is hardly in his grave, and already Betty is redoing the house. She had it repainted a God-awful tacky shade of green and ripped out my mom's favorite wallpaper in the kitchen to replace it with some cheap wood paneling. Can you believe she would do this without even asking us?" As Mr. Masseuse relayed his disgust about seeing the vacation home overrun and revamped by his stepfamily, he became increasingly oblivious to my painful moans and requests for a gentler touch on my back. Finally, only after I let out a sharp scream, did he come to his senses and change the subject.

ON A WING AND A PRAYER

Later that afternoon as I taxied to Dulles International Airport, I befriended cab driver Bill. He had been happily married for seventeen years to his high school sweetheart and had two teenaged girls. Stuck in traffic, the conversation eventually got around to what I do, and upon telling him, Bill said he was embarrassed to admit that he and his wife didn't have wills. Yes, years ago they had met with a lawyer to discuss their estate planning, but he and his wife had been unable to agree on guardianship. The grandparents on both sides were either deceased or too old to take on the emotional and financial responsibilities of raising children. Siblings on both sides of their families always seemed mired in some sort of distress—from bankruptcy to divorce to delinquent kids, not to mention questionably-behaving second wives and husbands. When I asked about friends as potential guardians, Bill said, "Outside the family? My sister would die if we did that. She'd never forgive me." Their solution, given the unlikelihood that anything would happen to both of them, was simple: Leave it in God's hands. As we reached the airport and I got out of the car, he turned and asked, "Is it possible to put *that* in a will?"

What These Three Stories
(and Thousands More)
Share in Common

Unlike the focus of most estate planning today, *none of these stories has anything to do with taxes*. The real issues behind wills gone wrong—or wills that get started but sidelined—are the *human* ones. When sticky family dynamics have been left unaddressed, wills become ticking time bombs. Just ask anyone in the wake of a parent's death. Chances are slim that you'll hear about siblings squabbling over some fancy tax shelter or the Rule Against Perpetuities. No, they are fighting over Dad's Sears Craftsman power tools, Grandma's engagement ring, or whether to replace the orange shag carpet in the home they just inherited together. They are fighting over the deceased's choice of a guardian or why one of them was named an executor and the others kids were "left out." They are fighting over different perceptions of equity and often simply their memories or your love. They are fighting over the communication blind spots that wills rarely address, because we are too distracted by tax codes or legal requirements when creating them. And when you throw in stepfamilies, blended families, scattered-across-the-country families, and families headed by unmarried partners, even the most loving clan can explode. Worse yet, you are no longer there to untangle the mess. In fact, your legacy becomes the mess!

Stumbling Blocks

Wills that *don't* work place too much consideration on the legal and financial laws of distribution at the expense of the human ones. They fail to consider the impact of estate planning decisions on loved ones. They end up being a piece of paper left in a drawer or with the lawyer, rather than becoming a heartfelt communication tool—a compass that can guide your family to a greater sense of emotional and financial well-being once you are gone. No wonder so many people lose their "will" power when it comes to starting and completing the estate planning process.

So, how did we get here? When did the technical and legal side take the estate planning process hostage? Why do so many estate planning books start with a glossary of legal terms, tax planning structures, and balance sheets? While of course these issues are important and will be discussed in this book, we've ended up where we are today because for many advisors it's easier to manage finances rather than family feelings; deal with county, state, and federal estate taxes rather than taxing family situations; and talk valuables rather than personal values. Further, they are left to grapple with the complexities and configurations of modern families using a legal system dating back to medieval English times when sheep were the likely property and women were called chattel.

Finding Your "Will" Power

In the course of my work, I have asked thousands upon thousands of men and women if they have a will. What I frequently hear is that many don't have one at all, or started but got stuck, or finishing it was pushed aside by the daily rigors of life—from career-climbing to child-rearing. Sometimes they even admit that a completed will has been sitting on their desk for weeks—and even months—but that they just haven't had time to review and sign it. A 30-something investment banker and father of three whom I met in passing—and who later died in the World Trade Center terrorist attacks—said just that to me only a few months before 9/11. His kind face and that brief conversation we had about his will have haunted me to this day. I often pray that he finally got around to signing it, sparing his wife and three young daughters further pain and hardship.

Yes, it's true, most of us find developing a will about as enticing as cleaning out the basement or garage. Wills are about death. Wills are about taxes and complicated legal/financial things. And wills involve facing emotionally charged family issues and dilemmas that are like quicksand: Should I leave more money to my struggling daughter with three kids than my successful investment banker son? Can I trust my four children to take care of their disabled brother if I leave them all the money? Should I give as much to my stepchildren, whom I adore, as I do to my biological children? What will my well-off children say if I leave all or most of my money to charity? Why should I bother leaving money to a daughter who refuses to speak to me? If we don't ask a grandmother the kids can't stand to be their guardian, will she be hurt if we just make her the backup guardian? Can I pass on my favorite antiques to one daughter who will appreciate them more than the others and has the space in her home to accommodate them? Does it make sense to consider as part of my son's inheritance the enormous sums we spent sending him to medical school? What if I don't have anything of real financial value to leave to my family?

Like it or not, your will—or what the state determines if you don't have one (See side bar: What Happens to Your Family When You Die Without a Will?)—voices your final message to your loved ones, telling them not only *who gets what*, but also *who you are*. Wouldn't you rather that message reflect your real priorities in life, as well as what you most want for your loved ones after you are gone? Death naturally brings loved ones closer together. Don't let your will—or a lack of one—tear them apart.

The Essence of The Good Will Approach

For more than a decade, I have successfully practiced a revolutionary approach to estate planning that turns the process upside down—focusing first on the human issues before determining the technical, legal, and financial structures that will best address them. How well you understand the human side and incorporate it into your decision-making can make the difference between leaving a legacy of warmed hearts or heated heads.

Many mistakenly think that estate plans are only for great Gatsby types. But you don't need a mansion or millions of dollars to need an estate plan! Throughout this book, estate planning simply refers to the process of determining your last wishes regarding both values and valuables, making arrangements for the care of your dependents, and determining what should happen to you and your resources if you become incapacitated during your lifetime. Regardless of the value of your assets, your decisions about these matters will greatly affect your family long after you are gone. Estate planning allows you to make choices for yourself, rather than letting the state decide for you. The will itself is the legal centerpiece of any estate plan. It documents your wishes for the distribution of assets and allows you to nominate a guardian for

WHAT HAPPENS TO YOUR FAMILY WHEN YOU DIE WITHOUT A WILL?

It is estimated that seven out of ten Americans today have no will, and the 30 percent who do, don't keep the document up to date. When you die without a will, a probate court must appoint a representative for your estate. Yes, everyone has an estate, not just wealthy people. An estate is essentially all your possessions—any assets that are in your name, including your part of those you co-own with a spouse or other party. When the court does this, your case is labeled "intestate," a fancy way of saying that the state steps in and decides who gets what for you. In the midst of grieving over their loss, your family is left holding the bag for this time-consuming process that often drags on for months, if not years. It can also be an expensive drain on their finances, significantly shrinking the benefits of the estate. Costs for a lawyer, bonds, inventory, and accounting (which a will could have prevented) are likely to be incurred.

As a result of this lack of "will" power, your loved ones are required to bring a lawsuit against the state to ask the probate judge to transfer your assets from you to them. *Is this really the graceful exit and last impression you intend?*

Each state has it own formula for distribution. Sometimes half the assets go to the spouse and half to your children. Sometimes your spouse only gets a third. Without a will, people who aren't

your children. But a will is only one piece of the puzzle and is augmented by a number of other, equally important components that we will discuss later in this book—living wills, legacy vehicles, trusts, health care proxies, and durable powers of attorney. (See sidebar: The Good Will Approach: Nuts and Bolts Definitions.)

related by blood to you are most likely out of luck altogether, including stepchildren whom you care for but have not formally adopted or a live-in partner. Yes, you could live with someone for ten years without being married, and the court might decide to transfer your assets to a blood relative in Fargo you've never met instead of the most precious person in your life. It all depends on the state in which you reside. If you don't have any living family members who fall under the intestate laws where you live, the state can deem itself the only beneficiary and get everything!

When you have children under the age of 18 or other dependents, the will also designates who should care for them. Do you want your kids to be raised by an irresponsible aunt they can't stand? Do you want the state to decide who will care for an adult offspring with special needs?

And what about all of your other personal possessions—that baseball signed by Babe Ruth or your stamp collection worth a small fortune? You may have every intention of leaving them to someone special, but without a will the court might sell off your personal possessions in an estate sale so money can be distributed, forcing relatives to "buy back" family heirlooms. Even your beloved pet won't be spared from the fallout of not having a will. A will also gives you the opportunity to direct funds to a person for the care of Spot, Kitty, or your pet lizard Leonard for the rest of their lives.

Throughout the estate planning process, the Good Will approach puts a premium on recognizing the very real and powerful human dimensions at play that need consideration whether you've been avoiding writing a will, are looking for ideas on how to get started or unstuck, have created one without fully considering its impact on your family, are dreading the conflicts waiting in the wings

THE GOOD WILL APPROACH:
NUTS AND BOLTS DEFINITIONS

The terms used in estate planning are confusing to everyone! So here are some key definitions that will help to make things clearer. I will provide you with more of these as we go along.

Estate Planning: The process of determining your last wishes regarding both values and valuables, making arrangements for the care of your dependents, and determining what should happen to you and your resources if you become incapacitated during your lifetime. Ultimately, estate planning lets you make these choices for yourself, rather than leaving it to the state to decide.

Executor: Person or financial institution you name to carry out the terms of your will. Duties include paying debts, collecting property, filing taxes and forms, and distributing your possessions in accordance with your will. If you choose to have more than one, each is called a **Co-Executor.** Some states refer to a female executor as an **Executrix.** A **Successor Executor** is someone you choose to act as executor if the first-named person cannot serve.

Guardian: Person designated in the will to take on physical custody of—and/or property management for—a minor (in most states children under the age of 18 years old) or other dependent unable to care for themselves. Most guardians serve the dual role of both caring for the individual and managing assets. Someone who only manages the property, without physical custody of the child or other dependent, can also be called a **Conservator** or **Guardian of the Estate.** As with the executor, most lawyers will request a fallback candidate for the guardian and conservator.

Legacy Vehicles: Providing an opportunity to express things that aren't addressed in your will, legacy vehicles are a means of passing on your guiding values, beliefs, personal insights, and reflections in addition to communicating to loved ones why you have made the choices you have made in the estate plan. They are also known as ethical wills, legacy statements, family mission statements, living letters, life stories, personal histories, wish lists, or precatory letters. Whatever the name, they can range from a few paragraphs to multiple pages to bound volumes, and be video- or audiotaped. Although legacy vehicles are separate from your will and qualitative, rather than objectively quantifiable or legally enforceable, they are essential to creating goodwill.

Living Will: Not a will as most of us know it, but rather a legal document that lets you state the terms under which you no longer would want medical treatment (that is, no artificial life supports in the case of a terminal illness or serious accident), allowing doctors to comply with your predetermined wishes. **A Durable Healthcare Power of Attorney** (or **Healthcare Proxy**) extends the living will by allowing you to authorize a person to make medical decisions for you if you become incapacitated.

Power of Attorney: Allows you to give another person the power to take certain actions or make decisions on your behalf, generally healthcare or financial ones, under certain circumstances. A **Durable Power of Attorney** gives them the right to continue doing these actions even if you become incapacitated. Although the person you name is called an attorney-in-fact, they needn't be an attorney at all and could be your spouse, an adult child, a relative, or trusted friend.

Trust: Contained in the will itself or written as a separate document, a trust sets up a relationship in which one person manages property for the benefit of another who actually owns it, the **Beneficiary.** There are many types of trusts, under all sorts of complicated names, and they can appear rather confusing. The whole trust concept is best visualized as a legal box in which you store the assets you want to give people or organizations at a later time. You choose when and how. Then, you select the person(s) and/or financial institution(s)—called the **Trustee(s)**—who will hold the box, keep its contents safe, and handle its legal/financial management. You also choose when and for what reasons the trustee can open the box and release assets to the beneficiaries. At any given time, all trusts are either irrevocable or revocable. An irrevocable trust cannot be changed after it is set up. A revocable trust, such as a living trust, can be changed after it has been established. Most revocable trusts become irrevocable at some later time; for example, when the person who sets up the trust dies.

Will: The legal centerpiece of any estate plan, the will contains a cluster of decisions that include who gets what (people, trusts, charities), when and in what form (outright or held in trust), who carries out your wishes (executor, trustee), who cares for and/or manages the property of your dependents (guardian, conservator), and what happens to your body (burial and funeral instructions, organ donations).

when a loved one dies, or are already experiencing the aftermath. It will show you how to start with your values, consider your relationships, and improve communication with loved ones. It will equip you with a clearer understanding of the nuts and bolts of estate planning. It will provide you with the do's and don'ts to use when evaluating the trade-offs involved in making a variety of critical decisions.

And to make it even simpler, the Good Will approach is organized into what I call the seven *human* laws of distribution. Once these laws are taken into account, making choices that satisfy the legal and financial end of things becomes a fairly uncomplicated task. So before you attempt to fill out even that first form handed to you by the attorney or on the estate planning CD loaded on your computer, first consider the human laws of distribution, which are presented as the chapters of this book, as follows:

HUMAN LAW ONE

Consider Your Values   Although an afterthought in the traditional estate planning process, passing on your values, beliefs, and guiding principles is the most important thing you can do for yourself and loved ones. This chapter helps you to identify your values, then shows how to use them as the foundation for leaving your valuables. I will introduce a variety of legacy vehicles, tools for expressing what you stand for, your life's purpose, and how you want to be remembered—whether you have amassed substantial material assets or none at all.

Now that you've had a chance to begin identifying what's most important to you, do you know what's important to your family? As vital as your values are in guiding the development of your inheritance plan, equally necessary is facing the facts about the people who will most likely be sharing it.

HUMAN LAW TWO

Face Family Dynamics: It's Not Just About the Money Who are the players in your own circle of loved ones and how do they get along with you and each other? What are their expectations when it comes to your estate? This chapter asks you to take an honest look at your family and its dynamics before developing the inheritance plan they will someday be sharing. Wills frequently bring unfulfilled emotional needs and unresolved hurts to the surface. Money and "who gets what" often symbolize other issues that have little to do with the stuff itself—from parental favoritism to sibling rivalry, from expectations to entitlement, from childhood memories to proof of love and acceptance. In this chapter, I'll first ask you to determine who depends on you and any loved ones you intend to provide for in your absence. Then, I'll give you a set of questions to consider that will help assess the dynamics of your unique set of loved ones, including life stages and circumstances, relationships with you and among each other, expectations and assumptions regarding your inheritance plan, money values, and what's really important to your family.

Once you've begun to take an honest look at your family and considered their relationships, money values, and differing needs and expectations, it's time to take stock of all the stuff.

HUMAN LAW THREE

Start with the Small Stuff, Then On to the Big Stuff
When inventorying what you have to pass on, start with the small stuff before moving to the big stuff. From family heirlooms, furniture, and photos to that special wedding band or holiday recipe file, the small stuff often has the potential to create the most hostility and division in a family. This chapter provides food for thought and offers creative distribution solutions for emotionally charged possessions that can be employed now and later to create goodwill. Then I will lay the groundwork for thinking about what you have to leave when it comes to the big stuff—your home, insurance policies, retirement accounts, 401(k)s, and more—from methods of inventorying what you have to whose name is on the title, from when you need to worry about taxes to which assets will go through pro-

bate. By the end of this chapter, you'll begin to see a much clearer picture of what you have as you continue to think about what you might want to do with it.

Once you've taken stock of your stuff, large and small, and before you make any final decisions on what you want to do with it, it's time to think about putting your team in place.

HUMAN LAW FOUR

It's Football, Not Fishing . . . So Build a Team You Can Trust   Attorney. Executor. Trustee. Personal and property guardians for your minor children or adult offspring with disabilities. Attorney-in-fact for advanced financial and healthcare directives including living wills. The titles and roles of the estate team can all get very confusing. Worse yet, many of these roles overlap, making it hard to keep straight who does what and the decision-making for selecting each exponentially harder. Yet these people whom you entrust with your life, your children, and your wishes are crucial to creating and maintaining peace in your family as well as keeping your estate plan intact. To help you sort through the maze, this chapter describes the roles and responsibilities of each and addresses the most common questions and concerns people have when putting together their team. Every section ends with a checklist of questions to ask yourself or potential candidates before making a nomination.

Once you've thought about who you want to help carry the ball and which of your loved ones to involve, it's time to consider two other distribution dilemmas you might confront, beginning with issues of fairness.

HUMAN LAW FIVE

Recognize That Fair Is Not Always Equal   To keep the peace, should you treat all heirs the same? In your circle of loved ones, are some depending on you more than others? If your partner has children from a previous marriage, do you leave them an inheritance equal to your own children? Is it fair to leave more to your daughter who chose to be a schoolteacher and still needs the down payment for a house than to a thriving investment banker son with money to burn? While equalization sounds simple on paper, you and your family members will each have your own perceptions of what is fair and equal. In the end, the decision is yours. This chapter highlights a variety of fairness dilemmas and how each family came to grips with the problems they were facing. I'll also give you the tools to address issues in your own family.

Once you've come to grips with your own family fairness issues, you might also want to consider the implications—and wisdom—of using your will to address unfinished business with a significant loved one.

HUMAN LAW SIX

Unleash the Power of Forgiveness   When a relationship with a son, daughter, or grandchild goes through rocky times, what sometimes runs through people's minds is this: "I'm going to cut you from my will. You'll never see a cent." But before acting on thoughts like these, hold on! If you're thinking of cutting a child out of your estate— or using your will to make a point about an unresolved relationship—think again. This chapter covers the legal issues, the emotional repercussions, and ultimately suggests why the greatest gift is to make peace now—not only for your heir, but even more importantly for yourself.

Once you've made choices about what to leave and how to leave it, it's time to get everyone on the same page. Have you found ways to let your loved ones know why you made those choices? If not, you are setting them up for grief gridlock!

HUMAN LAW SEVEN

It's Not What You Say, It's How You Say It ... and Whether You Bother to Say It at All   If you haven't noticed already, communication is everything, yet it remains one of the biggest obstacles to the successful development and implementation of any estate plan. Here you'll find a variety of innovative communication vehicles and troubleshooting tips—from ways to get the family together to discuss the issue to how much you should share about the details of your estate, from broaching your mortality with your children to addressing the sensitive subject with your parents in order to prevent inheriting your own set of conflicts. Here I'll share tools and techniques that have helped my clients create goodwill in their own families throughout the estate planning process.

Once you've given these seven laws full attention, you'll be well on your way to creating the Good Will!

Creating
The Good Will

HUMAN LAW ONE
Consider Your Values

In 1888, when Swedish inventor Alfred Nobel—best known at the time for creating dynamite and nitroglycerin—lost his brother in France, the French newspaper made a horrible mistake and ran the obituary for Alfred instead. With a headline proclaiming "The Merchant of Death is Dead!," the obituary credited Alfred with creating the most destructive weapon known to mankind and lining his pockets by enabling people to kill one another more quickly and in greater numbers than ever before.

As Alfred read the obituary, horror and shock were added to his grief. There was no mention of his hundreds of more benign patented inventions or his profound interest in social issues. For the first time, Alfred saw himself as the world did and vowed not to go down in history as the Merchant of Death.

From that day forward, emboldened with changing his legacy from bombmaker to peacemaker, Alfred became a different man. Upon his death eight years later, he left his entire nine-million-dollar fortune to fund awards for those whose work would benefit humanity, not extinguish it. The rest is history. Now, more than one hundred years after his bequest, the annual Nobel honors in the fields of chemistry, physics, medicine, and literature—as well as, of course, the coveted Nobel Peace Prize—are the most well-known awards in the world. Ask anyone what he remembers of Alfred Nobel today, and you will be hard pressed to hear that he was the inventor of TNT.

While few of us will read our own obituaries or amass the amount of wealth and worldwide fame that Alfred Nobel did, what you do and *don't* consider during estate planning will ultimately speak volumes about you as a person. That's why the Good Will approach relies on your values to guide and shape the decisions that you must make throughout the process.

What's Missing from Most Estate Plans Today

Years ago, one of the most important parts of a will was the publicly read preamble—the last declaration of the deceased person's beliefs. The preamble expressed to both family and friends, "This is what the life I lived was all about and what I considered most important." Today, however, walk into almost any lawyer's office to discuss your will, and chances are the focus will be on the value of your bank accounts, not on your personal values. You'll be handed an extensive form to fill out with questions about your assets, number of dependents, and tax situation. Chances are slim that you'll also be asked up front any of the following:

- What are your three greatest hopes in life?
- What are your values and beliefs, financial and otherwise?
- What are your three greatest wishes for loved ones?

- What would you most like people to know about you?
- If you were to die tomorrow, how would you want to be remembered?

Try asking yourself these questions first—before developing your will—and suddenly the task is no longer just about the numbers, technical terminology, and tax codes. It stops being that necessary evil you grudgingly undergo, pass on to your spouse to figure out, or hand over to the attorneys and other advisors. Rather, it becomes a personal journey—a celebration of life—allowing you to imbed your wisdom into everything that you leave.

By encouraging a process of self-examination that helps to clarify what you want to do and why you want to do it, the Good Will approach leverages personal values and beliefs in two critical ways:

- First, your values become a compass for developing the estate plan. By reflecting on what you most want to accomplish with your will, your choices will be based on a series of value judgments—*not* just the latest tax codes—and on your own goals, rather than on someone else's well-intentioned guesses about what would be best for your family. As you will see from this chapter, if you are not clear up front on what is important to you, then someone else will make these critical decisions for you—*planting the seeds for trouble down the road.*

- And second, as you complete or revise your estate plan, the Good Will approach encourages you to draw on your values again—this time to express the thought process behind your choices, using a variety of legacy vehicles which will be discussed later in this chapter.

In most estate plans today, value and legacy expressions are either skipped altogether or developed, not as a starting point, but as an afterthought—after the will and other components are put into place. As well, many people mistakenly believe that discussions about values and legacy are reserved for the wealthy—those with sizeable estates who want to set up a charitable foundation, house their art collection, or donate a wing in their name to their alma mater. The truth is, whether your means are modest or substantial, your values can be used to weave the fabric of your will.

Who Ever Knew: The Importance of Communicating Values Up Front

My dear friend Sarah's mother, Janet, was in her final days of life, succumbing to a nine-year battle with breast cancer. While Janet's will, which focused primarily on divvying up assets among her three children, was in place and had been discussed with each of them, she had never thought to reveal an important detail about her values to her family. At least not until the day she overheard a conversation her daughter was having regarding the funeral arrangements.

Janet heard Sarah say that in lieu of flowers, contributions should be made to a certain breast cancer research institute in honor of her mother. Sarah and her siblings had assumed Janet would have wanted this. In fact, Janet preferred that contributions in her memory went to support the passion of her life, rather than something associated with the cause of her death. Janet asked Sarah to request that contributions be made to the library at the local elementary school, where she had been volunteering for years by reading to the third and fourth graders each week. She went on to explain, much to the surprise of her daughter, that it would give her great pleasure to see the money used to buy some extra books for the children.

"How come I didn't know that about my mother?" asked Sarah when we met for lunch, a few months after the funeral. Then she told me that, not only did they deliver on Janet's request—initially providing a check of more than $2,000 for book purchases—but they had also set up a memorial fund to provide money for books each year. To show its appreciation, the school dedicated an entire section of the library in their mother's honor. Sarah described how fulfilling it had been to visit the library and see a plaque reading: THE JANET A. MILLER READING ROOM.

As Sarah remarked, "As part of her will, I never even considered asking my mom about the values and legacy she wanted to pass on. In many ways, I thought it went without saying." Sarah explained how her mom had been a model parent, providing endless support and encouragement to her family. She hoped to emulate Janet one day when she had kids of her own. Even in the face of death, constantly battling breast cancer, Janet had always looked on the bright side. Her unwavering optimism was a legacy that Sarah said she would draw strength from when faced with life's challenges. "But I have to tell you, Elizabeth," Sarah concluded, "seeing my mom's spirit carried forward in that little reading room has given my brothers and me more comfort than we ever imagined possible."

What Are Values?

Values are anything you believe is important in life: family, a home, achievement, spirituality, community service, education, self-sufficiency, financial independence, financial security, peace of mind, helping others, a good marriage, and so on. Unconsciously shaped by our upbringing and experiences, values often change over time as we mature and enter different life phases. A young hard-driving entrepreneur's need for financial gain and recognition in his field may well give way to a desire to support charitable causes in his later years. Beliefs, attitudes, and behaviors are the barometer of our values. The best way to clarify your values is to start by asking yourself the following:

- What is most important to me in life?
- What do I stand for and believe in?
- What truly matters to me?
- How do I want to be remembered?
- What is my life legacy and how do I want it to be celebrated?

Now, discuss your thoughts with a trusted loved one. As you go through this process, be sure to be honest with yourself! Once you've identified your values, you will be able to start reflecting them in your estate planning. And by communicating your hopes and dreams, your heirs will be better able to carry them forward. Consider these two examples.

Ruth, a 65-year-old widow with five adult children and ten great-grandchildren, ranked absolutely top of the list: self-sufficiency, independence, and a home; specifically this meant the ability to care for herself as long as possible and to remain in the cozy retirement cottage that she and her husband had purchased before his death. It wasn't that her family was unimportant, but a deep commitment to self-reliance far outweighed her desire to insure that offspring were left with as much financial security as possible. How did Ruth's values ultimately shape her estate plan? Instead of depleting her assets through substantial tax-savings gifts to her children as recommended by her accountant, she chose to keep the money. This allowed her to live comfortably in the present and to ensure a self-sufficient, independent style into the foreseeable future. Besides, Ruth reasoned, giving them the money now to save on taxes might backfire. Down the road, if her resources became depleted, she could become a burden to her children who might have already spent the assets she gifted to them earlier on. Before making any final decisions, Ruth spoke to her children about what she was thinking. She was pleasantly surprised to hear that, while they certainly could all use the money, it was far more important to them that she lived out her final years as happy and independently as possible. As one of her sons added, "It just wouldn't be the same if the family couldn't enjoy the annual trek to Grandma's home each Christmas. It means so much to me and the kids. I'll take that and the memories over the money any day."

Martin, 54, and Theresa, 44, have been married for nine years and have one son, who is eight years old. Before they met, they worked for many years in the corporate world. For most of their married life, each has been gainfully self-employed: Martin as a freelance documentary filmmaker and Theresa as an independent marketing consultant. They both work from home in the hills of North

Carolina and estimate that their estate—between pensions, 401(k)s, home, land, and cash accounts—is worth more than a million dollars. Incredibly, they don't have a will!

When I asked them separately to write down what was most important to them, each ranked top on their list: financial security for their son and giving back to the community. On the financial security front, both had worked hard all their lives and remarked that they had wished their own parents had given them a financial head start in life. So it was important to them to give their son a leg up. However, when I dug deeper into how they envisioned doing just that in a will, two very distinct pictures emerged. Theresa insisted that their son be given all the money in one lump-sum payout when he was of age, no strings attached, so he would have the full resources to pursue any career of his choosing without worrying about paying the rent. Martin, on the other hand, felt it was absolutely vital to instill a strong work ethic in his son, and so preferred the funds be distributed at key life turning points.

How did Martin's and Theresa's different perceptions of the same value ultimately affect this part of their estate plan? They came to a compromise by setting up a trust that gave their son enough money for education and living expenses at age 18, and the rest when certain milestones were achieved, such as completing a college education and working for a certain number of years.

On the giving back to the community front, the couple was sure they wanted to leave something to the town in which they resided. However, they were not sure exactly what that should be. Digging deeper, asking them what was really important to them, I found that they were both very committed to land conservation. In the end, they decided to bequeath ten acres of their land to the community for the purpose of developing a town park with a play-ground and walking trails. They named their son to over-see the park's development when he came of age.

In the end, Theresa and Martin developed a video for their son explaining the thought process behind their estate plan. In addition to talking about the conditions for his inheritance, the video also captured them walking the family land, pointing out where and for what reasons they had planted certain things, and why they had chosen the particular ten-acre track to gift to the town. By following the Good Will approach, their estate plan reflected the core values that were important to each of them, leaving their son with a legacy that would endure and give him great comfort long after they were gone.

Bedroom Accords: It Takes Two

As the previous example underscores, the same values can mean very different things to two individuals, even to those who have been married for many years. Flushing out your values, attitudes, and beliefs before you begin developing a will and the other essential components of your estate plan is as important as getting both heads of household involved in the first place.

Sadly, however, this is rarely the case. Frequently, one partner leaves it to the other to deal with the will and the rest of that "financially challenging stuff." And with married couples from the older generations, that missing link is most often the wife. This is what I hear from those clients: "My wife doesn't want to be involved in any of this—she says she has sat through enough meetings discussing our finances. It just doesn't interest her." Or this:

"My wife says that as long as it's clear that her sister will take care of the kids, she doesn't want to be involved in anything else concerning our will."

Sometimes these wives will sit out of discussions regarding the estate because they feel they aren't heard and their opinions are ignored. This is often the case when husbands have dominating personalities, or are simply operating out of expectations from their upbringing. When the wife tries to offer her views and perspective, they are flatly discounted with quick reactions and counter opinions from the husband. After being ignored and overpowered, she simply gives up, often not having the heart to share the truth: It's not because she isn't interested, it's because her views aren't valued.

As times change, with banker wives earning more and being more financially knowledgeable than their artist husbands—or with same-gender partners—the above scenarios are increasingly played out in a variety of new ways. But in all cases, getting in touch with feelings—not just finances—is an essential prerequisite to making important decisions that will affect the family for decades to come. And as you can see, the Good Will approach asks each person to plug into both heart and head. Bringing together the logical and emotional perspective provides balance. When people start synthesizing their thinking with their feelings, they create a whole much greater than the parts and are able to produce incredible results. Having a values discussion up front will inevitably lead couples to recall their formative years: how they met, what they share in common, how they are different and complement each other, how they've overcome challenges, and how they feel about their children, if any. This process often brings them closer together and is one of the many great side benefits of following the Good Will approach! (See sidebar: Just Say No to a Twofer.)

So, the next time you experience resistance when trying to get your partner involved, ask these questions:

- "Do you mean to tell me that *you,* who knows our children so well and loves them so very much, do not want to provide any input into what each should receive and how best to structure that inheritance to keep the family peace?"

- "Do you mean that *you,* who has worked so hard and made so many sacrifices to keep us all happy and to help create a loving home, are not interested in putting into place something that encapsulates our wisdom and values and seeing our shared legacy live on?"

- "Do you mean that *you,* someone who is so involved in the community, has absolutely no interest in helping to decide whether some of your money will go to a charity and, if so, which one?"

Try it. These questions work every time to bring both the heart *and* head of each partner into the fold.

Legacy Vehicles

Legacy vehicles are a way for you to pass on your values and to communicate to your loved ones why you have made the choices you have made in your estate plan. They give you the opportunity also to express things that aren't addressed in your will. Legacy expressions often serve as the glue that binds families together, particularly in times of grief and hardship, or when children start to quibble over the fine print in your will. Legacy vehicles are most

JUST SAY NO TO A TWOFER

Two people can create a single will document, called a joint will. Married couples might view this as a more efficient or cost-effective option. However, unless your attorney has a very clear and specific reason for suggesting a joint will for your particular situation, just say no. In most cases, drawing up two separate wills is the better option.

Some states treat a joint will like a contract. Once one person dies, the estate plan is locked in, preventing the surviving spouse from making any changes to the will. With a joint will, if the surviving partner tries to modify anything, the beneficiaries—who might get less after changes—are likely to contest. Kaboom. There goes the family.

Although separate wills cost only marginally more than a joint will, they give you and your spouse the freedom to adapt to life changes. What if unforeseen events mean your spouse needs more from the estate than originally anticipated? What if your daughter's marriage is in trouble and your spouse can't take steps to protect her share from that son-in-law you never quite liked? What if your house becomes so valuable after you are gone that an entirely different plan might save a huge amount in taxes for your spouse?

Joint wills also can create other tax problems. If a husband and wife choose voluntarily to give each other things, there is no

commonly completed in the form of what is known today as an ethical will. However, they are sometimes also called legacy statements, family mission statements, living letters, life stories, personal histories, wish lists, or precatory letters. (See sidebar: Two Examples of Legacy Expressions.) Whatever the name, they can range from a few paragraphs to multiple pages to bound volumes. For those who find the written word limiting, or prefer another form, they can also be video- or audiotaped.

tax (called the marital deduction in estate tax). If, however, a joint will is found to be a contract, the survivor might not receive his or her own belongings tax free. Yikes. In this case, you would be better off with no will at all.

On a more personal note, you and your spouse have different property—things like jewelry or treasured golf clubs. Not only will each of you learn about what's most important to you when creating your own lists of specific gifts for separate wills, but you'll also have the opportunity to learn what's most important to the other.

If you and your spouse agree to give everything to each other for your lifetime and then pass it on to your children, you can just say so in your own wills. On the other hand, if you want to be certain about what happens to your assets after you pass on, you can create a trust. State laws and personal circumstances will affect how to address these and other issues regarding property and common interests (such as guardianship of children) in your separate wills. Each will should also include a clause stating what happens if you and your spouse die at the same time.

Finally, we all want to leave our mark in the world. Having a personal will gives you the freedom to write certain things exactly how you want and to take responsibility for your own choices.

Legacy vehicles are different from wills as most people know them. Whereas your will is a legally binding and enforceable document that essentially instructs how assets will be distributed and divided after you die, legacy vehicles are nonlegally binding and unenforceable expressions that pass on to loved ones your guiding principles, ideals, beliefs, and other personal insights or reflections. Although legacy vehicles are separate from your will and qualitative, rather than objectively quantifiable or legally enforceable, they are essential to creating the Good Will.

TWO EXAMPLES OF LEGACY EXPRESSIONS

Dear John, Ellyn, and Ann,

I can't believe that I have hit the big six-five! While Dr. Wilson says I am in fine shape for a man my age, I know that with retirement from my insurance company looming, I am entering the twilight years of my life.

I want you to know that I am NOT disappointed that you chose other career paths than working for the firm. While it would have been wonderful to see your smiling faces every day, I am so very proud of how each of you has walked to the beat of your own drum—John as a master carpenter, Ellyn as a superb writer, and Ann as a full-time mom.

As you know, I have never been one to wear my emotions on my sleeve, but I hope you will take with you what I have valued most in my life: a loving family that sticks together through thick and thin (at no time did I see that more than when your mom passed last year), a marriage (or relationship, for you John who has yet to tie the knot!) based on mutual respect and appreciation, and taking the time to enjoy the finer things in life.

As you know, one of my greatest pleasures in life has been the cabin on Lake George. If I have one request, it's that the three of you keep it and continue to enjoy it. In addition to the other assets I have left to each of you, I've set aside a fund that should be more than enough to help in the cabin's upkeep. Some of my most cherished moments with Mom and you kids were at Lake George—fishing, taking catnaps on the dock, sailing, and those long family dinners on the porch. I hope as the years unfold you will continue those traditions among yourselves and with your circle of loved ones.

I love you all,
Dad

LAST WISHES IN YOUR OWN WORDS

The beauty of legacy vehicles is that you can express yourself in your own words. Unlike the will, which contains pages and pages of often dry and sterile legalese written by

Dear Matt, Silvia, Jessica, Ryan, and Laura,

I know the fastest way to your hearts has always been through food—not only from eating it, but the times we've enjoyed together in the kitchen making holiday cookies and preparing for special occasions from Thanksgiving to graduation celebrations.

I don't need to tell you how much I love to cook and bake, but the real joy of it has always been spending time with all of you and gathering around the table.

You probably never realized how happy it has made me over the years when I get your calls and e-mails, asking, "Grandma, I am having people over, remind me again, how do you make your . . . ?" You'll never know how much this has tickled me.

So I want to make sure that after I am gone, and won't be here to answer your questions, you'll always have my love and recipes nearby. I've put together a little booklet for each of you with all the family favorites, including my banana bread.

You may not know this, but some of these recipes have their origins in my own grandmother's kitchen—though I'll confess, I have changed many of them over the years. Don't be afraid to experiment! I am sure you'll make these recipes even better, just as you'll do with everything else in your lives. All I ask in return is that each of you promise to pass on your own versions of these recipes to your grandchildren when the time comes.

All My Love,
Grandma Pat

an estate attorney, the contents and length of legacy vehicles are limited only by one's imagination and are generally written by the person leaving the estate.

In addition to expressing the thinking behind your estate plan, legacy vehicles can also express life lessons, milestones, blessings, hopes and dreams for the future, and even regrets or apologies. Often they proclaim love for survivors; help to explain and reconcile past actions; recount life-changing experiences, events, or stories; and dispense advice reflecting deeply ingrained values and beliefs.

For example, one of my clients was bestowing a large part of her wealth to a charitable organization involved with land preservation for wildlife. She wrote a letter telling her children and grandchildren why this cause meant so much to her by relaying the story of her travels to Africa as a teenager with her father, where she saw families of elephants herded together and then murdered in cold blood by local hunters. Conveying the intimate and horrific details of her story to heirs was far more effective in insuring that her wishes would remain unchallenged than had she simply stated that X amount of dollars fund X charity. Another client wrote a letter to his children saying he regretted caving into the pressure from his parents to follow a more lucrative and upstanding career as a doctor, rather than building on his love of photography to pursue a career as a globetrotting photojournalist. He wrote, "While no doubt the career path I have followed has greatly benefited us all financially, one of the most important things in life is to have a passion for your work. As is often said, 'do what you love and the money will follow.' I wish I had taken that advice." Based on his own life experience and values, this client went a step further than just writing a letter. He created a trust in his will so that each child could take one great adventure or have seed money for starting a company.

The contents of legacy vehicles can be amended and added to during the course of one's life. Many people develop or revise them at major turning points. These can be transitional life stages—such as marriage, birth of children and grandchildren, facing their own or loved one's milestone birthdays, graduation, or even when the children start leaving for college and the empty nest sets in. They should also be modified when facing a challenging life situation such as divorce, the sickness or death of a loved one, trying financial times, and even when faced with the shock of current events, such as September 11, 2001. (See sidebar: A Few Do's and Don'ts for Developing Legacy Vehicles.)

Legacy expressions can also be passed on well before *you* pass on, if you so choose. In fact, sharing and discussing their contents often creates an opportunity to reach common ground with heirs and to preempt dissension that might ensue upon your death.

WE ALL HAVE SOMETHING TO PASS ON

Recently, I met two childhood friends whom I hadn't seen in years for a reunion lunch—two sisters in their thirties, Heather and Nancy. The sisters were raised in an upper middle class family with eight children, three boys and five girls. While growing up, their father was a force on the Chicago Board of Trade and the children reaped the financial rewards, from private schools and fine colleges to country clubs and shiny new cars. Yet, later in life, due to a variety of circumstances, their father lost most everything—including the sprawling midwestern family home. Shortly thereafter, the once-strong family unit unraveled. Their father had become bitter, their mother disengaged, and the siblings started feuding—the girls blamed the three oldest brothers for not coming to their dad's rescue and helping him get back on his feet as the sisters had in previous years.

When they asked what I was in town for, I explained. Heather said, "You know, my dad was diagnosed with

A FEW DO'S AND DON'TS FOR DEVELOPING LEGACY VEHICLES

Legacy expressions can cover all sorts of topics. The most important thing to remember when putting one together is this: The more loved ones know about you, the more they will be able to embrace and pass on your legacy and to respect your final wishes.

Do:

Outline Your Values. Express your hopes, dreams, and wishes for your circle of loved ones. Outline the beliefs and values that reflect your life and emphasize your desire to see that your heirs carry them into the future.

Reflect. Pass on your wisdom about life, success, struggles, relationships, and investment strategies. Share how you felt the day your children were born or tell them which of their accomplishments made you the most proud.

Express Love. Write about characteristics and traits that you most value in your loved ones and describe how these qualities have affected your life.

Clear the Air. Are there experiences that seriously affected your loved ones, either directly or indirectly, in which you wish to make amends? Don't be afraid to acknowledge your shortcomings and ask for forgiveness.

Give Thanks. Are there people in your life whom you wish to give thanks to and acknowledge specifically? A mentor who made a difference, a son or daughter who taught you a particularly wise lesson, a wife who gave you unwavering support during a difficult period? Take the opportunity to say so.

Review It Annually. Like your will and other components of your estate plan, review your legacy expressions annually or as your life circumstances change.

Don't:

Enter the Spin Zone. Think twice about imposing values that introduce unrealistic—or downright hypocritical—restrictions on your heir's behavior. People, even children, can spot an imposter in seconds. If you haven't practiced what you preach, don't expect your loved ones to happily embrace the values you pass down—at least not without a convincing explanation from you.

Play the Blame Game. Resist the urge to point fingers and condemn. No one will want to read about how disappointed you were with your delinquent son or how Uncle Mike was a do-nothing bum. Resolve these issues personally by addressing them now, one-to-one, ideally in person. Or skip to Human Law Six and consider the power of forgiveness!

Make Monetary Demands. One of the purposes of legacy vehicles is to ask that your values be considered, such as "I hope my tradition of supporting the local library will continue." Avoid statements such as, "It is my wish that $1,000 be given each year to the local library." Any specific dollar amounts for gifts that you wish to bequeath should be directly stated in your will.

---

early-stage prostate cancer two years ago. While his prognosis looks good, some days he doesn't feel so well. Naturally, alarm bells go off in our heads. When I finally got up the courage to ask my mom whether they had gotten their will and what-not sorted out, she said yes, but there wasn't a whole lot to pass on." Nancy chimed in, "You know, I can't believe he might die and leave us nothing—not so much in terms of the big stuff, I know most of that is long gone—but of himself. I mean, can't he at least find some way to reconcile what has happened over the years? It would be great if he could just tell us what we each meant to him, share stories about his life for the grandchildren, or maybe just talk about the importance of the family. This would be such a perfect time to mend fences and bring us all back together. But where in a will could he put any of that? Interestingly, when I recently mentioned to him that I had gone to D.C. on business, he asked if I knew he had been accepted on scholarship to the Naval Academy in Annapolis when he was young. I never heard that and bet there's so much more he has to share with us."

What Nancy was searching for from her father is very similar to what can be communicated in legacy vehicles. Think—are your loved ones in need of something similar from you? Even if you have nothing of great material substance to pass on, sometimes the greatest gift of all, the one with most value, is simply yourself.

Face Family Dynamics: It's Not Just About the Money

Now that you've considered what's important to *you*, do you know what's important to your family? While every family has things to be proud of, each one also has things they would rather not think about—and if your loved ones aren't getting along now, that's unlikely to suddenly change when they read your will. If anything—unless you take the realities of family dynamics into account when planning your estate—things will likely get worse. Wills frequently bring unfulfilled emotional needs and unresolved hurts to the surface. For many people, money and "who gets what" symbolize other issues that have little to do with the stuff itself—from parental favoritism to sibling rivalry, from expectations to entitlement, from childhood memories to differing perceptions of what's fair. What you leave your family members can all too easily become a surrogate for affection, acceptance, and proof of your love.

Who are the players in your own circle of loved ones

and how do they get along with you and each other? What are their expectations when it comes to your estate? Do you have a son-in-law who likes to take over or a daughter who has credit card problems? Have you and your spouse sent different messages to the children about fiscal responsibility? Before making decisions about who gets what, take an honest look at your family and its dynamics.

This chapter will first help you determine who depends on you and identify the people you intend to provide for in your absence. Then it will give you questions to assess the dynamics of your unique set of loved ones. These questions, divided into sections, will cover a number of aspects including life stages and circumstances, relationships with you and among each other, expectations and assumptions regarding your inheritance plan, money values, and what's really important to your family.

By thinking about these questions, you'll more clearly be able to consider your loved ones' differing needs and expectations when not only determining what to leave to whom, but also how to leave it in the most meaningful, memorable, and peace-making way.

Put On Your Binoculars and Check Out the Landscape

Whether you have a Norman Rockwell family or one that more closely resembles the current British royalty, every family marches to its own beat. Each and every family has its own unique dynamics that can wreak havoc on even the best laid inheritance plans. Believe me, you don't need any obvious signs of family strife or even a complicated situation to have family members quarrel with each other about how to sort out your estate.

To give you an idea of what can happen when family dynamics aren't taken into account, even with a relatively straightforward group, consider the Dyers and the unexpected rift created over what to do with the home the children inherited from their mother.

The immediate Dyer family includes three adult siblings, their spouses, and their four children. The family matriarch recently passed away and left to her adult children the beloved colonial-style residence on a tree-lined street that had been her home for more than three decades. As with any group of siblings, the Dyer children had had their share of squabbles growing up. However, for most of their adult lives they and their families had happily gotten along. Yet now with a house to share—and based on individual life stages and circumstances, an angle I'll ask you to consider later in this chapter when assessing your own family dynamics—each had entirely different ideas about what they wanted to do with the property.

Dan, the oldest, wanted it sold immediately. After his mother's death and anticipating the proceeds from her estate, he and his wife, pregnant with their third child, had already spent the money, so to speak. By stretching their finances to the limit, they had just paid for the down payment on their dream home and would need the proceeds from the sale of his mother's house very soon in order to really afford the purchase.

On the other hand, Mary, the middle child, wanted to keep the family home. First, as a single mother with two teenagers, she saw this as an opportunity to finally have her own house. Second, she had been very close to her mom and felt especially attached to the place where the family had spent some of its best years. Third, as Mary explained to the others, the house was located just on the outskirts of a popular beach community. It would be a great place for everyone to continue to gather for holidays and vacations. In fact, if she purchased it, Mary told her brothers she would make it available for siblings, spouses, nieces, and nephews to visit whenever they wished. The sticky point: Mary would need a couple of years to get the money together to buy out her brothers. Maybe it could be rented in the meantime as a vacation home. Would the brothers mind waiting?

This, of course, didn't quite work for Dan who needed the money right away and was feeling immense pressure from his pregnant wife. She not only wanted the cash, but also dreaded the hassle of co-owning the property with her in-laws in the midst of juggling two small children and a new baby. While Dan had adored his mother and had attachments to the old house himself, right now he had his own family to think about.

The last child, laid-back Simon, was somewhere in the middle. Essentially he could go either way, though the prospect of having some money to fund his next travel adventure was becoming more appealing by the minute.

After much back and forth, Mary succumbed to Dan's pressure and reluctantly agreed to put the home on the market, admitting that it might be tough—although as she made clear to everyone *not completely impossible*—with her income to ever get a mortgage. No sooner had they gotten past that touchy matter, however, than the siblings found themselves at odds with the next issue: how best to sell the house. Mary insisted that they take time to fix it up to garner top dollar. She also reasoned that this would allow all of them more time to grieve and to more leisurely sort through the house and equitably distribute the contents. Dan's wife was suspicious. She thought this was just a ploy for Mary to buy time. A man of few words, again Simon was somewhere in the middle.

Dan and his wife eventually got their way. Everyone agreed to immediately put the house on the market. Yet before they could even take a breath, another topic reared its head: Who would sell the property? Mary, explaining that she knew the house and neighborhood better than any Realtor, wanted to sell it herself "by owner." Plus, she reasoned, they would save quite a bit of money not having to pay a Realtor's commission. Dan and his wife, of course, wanted a well-connected Realtor who could flip the house fast. In fact, his wife had already lined one up. This time Simon finally piped up and sided with Dan, pleading to his sister that they "just move on and get this all over with." In the ensuing discussions Mary exploded, "You see, this is how it has always been. You two just steamroll over me! You don't really give a hoot about this family, do you? You don't really care about me either, do you?"

Before they knew it, the whole exchange came to a screeching halt. Days later, Mary pulled a Ryder truck up to the home, hauling away more than half of its contents and cleaning out most of the garage without notifying either of her brothers. Concluding that she was the only one with an apparent attachment to the house and its possessions, she saw no reason to consult further with either one of them. Now Dan, his wife, and Simon were really furious. Mary had crossed the line.

Did the house finally get sold? Yes. Have the brothers and Dan's family spoken to Mary and hers to this day? Barely. How could a loving gesture from a mother go so wrong with a family that once seemed so close? If the matriarch had only considered what was going on in her children's lives, she might have communicated her last wishes regarding the house in much more specific terms.

As you think about your will, keep in mind that your family doesn't need an already obvious problem to end up with a situation disturbingly similar to what Dan, Mary, and Simon faced. As you will read time and time again throughout this book, sometimes it only takes an inadvertent spark to burn down the forest. By considering the varying aspects and angles of your own family's dynamics as presented through the following questions, you'll recognize potential sources of problems now and be better able to prevent them from playing out later.

TAKING STOCK

Let's start by taking stock. Begin with the basics. Who are the people you will be leaving things to? With family configurations so varied today, needless to say, it's different for everyone and truth is often stranger than fiction.

1. Family Composition: Who's Involved in Yours?

- Do you have a spouse or domestic partnership and/or any former ones?
- Do you have any minor children? What are their ages?
- Do you have any stepchildren? When did they come into your life? Did/Do they live with you?
- Do you have adult children? What are their ages?
- Are any of your children married, divorced, or living with partners?
- Do you have grandchildren? What are their ages?
- Are your parents living? What is the status of their health?
- Do you have other people whom you are considering leaving anything to, such as nieces and nephews or beloved friends?

DRILLING DOWN TO WHAT
MATTERS THE MOST

Now that you've identified the people in your circle of loved ones, it's time to start thinking about their life stages and circumstances, their relationships with you and each other, their expectations and assumptions regarding your estate, their money values, and what's most important to them.

Some of the subsequent questions will apply to you and your family. Others won't. Whatever the case, as you review them, keep the following in mind:

- Try to clear your lens and see things as they are, even if it feels a bit uncomfortable. Remember, you are not alone. Even the most loving families face relationship challenges.
- Be sure to check your assumptions at the door. For example, do you look at your grown son and still see a five-year-old with a runny nose? It's important for you to really see your loved ones for who they are today.
- Never underestimate the influence of in-laws (or established partners) on your loved one's thinking. No person is an island. Sure, you instilled your ideals in your children while raising them. But now they share a life with a person whose hopes, dreams, and values stem from a completely different set of players and experiences. Your loved one is not only sleeping with their spouse or significant other, but they are also sleeping with that person's background and perspective.
- Don't let yourself be bullied or manipulated by badly behaving loved ones who squawk and scream the loudest. Look closely at what behavior you want to reward and what values you want your choices to support.

- Resist the temptation to manipulate loved ones to spend time with you by promising rewards after you are gone or threatening to cut them out of your estate.

2. Life Stages and Circumstances of Loved Ones

- Are all of your adult children self-supporting? If not, when might they be?
- Have each of your children/grandchildren completed their educations? If not, when might they be completed?
- Do you have any dependents with special needs?
- Do you have obligations to more than one family?
- Do you provide care and/or financial support to your parents?
- Do you receive care from your family members?
- Are your loved ones feeling pressured, crunched, or unhappy about any aspects of their lives?
- What do you think frustrates your loved ones right now in their lives?

3. Relationships with You and Each Other

- How do you and your loved ones get along with you and each other?
- Do you really know all of them? Is there someone you are estranged from?
- What do they talk about? What don't they talk about at all?
- What are people most likely to argue about at a family dinner?
- What stories are told at family gatherings and how do your different loved ones respond to them? (Hint:

Sometimes loved ones' responses, or lack of them, will speak volumes about how they feel and can identify areas of simmering tension.)

- Can your loved ones share their toys (whether they are age 5 or 55)?
- Have you ever been accused of playing favorites with your children?
- Has one child taken care of you/been more attentive than others?
- Do you feel you have more in common with some loved ones than others? Why?
- Do your children's spouses see eye to eye? (Not just husband to wife, but are there rivalries between in-laws? Think back to comments at family gatherings.)
- If stepparents are in the picture, do you and they see eye to eye?
- Do your children's spouses have unmet expectations about your children?

4. Relationship with Money

- What does money represent to your loved ones? What about to their spouses?
- How financially responsible are your loved ones? How well have they handled their own money and assets? (Hint: Look for patterns of interactions with money over time.)
- If you have a spouse or partner, do you handle money differently? Have you sent mixed messages about money to your children? (See sidebar: Raising Children to Be Responsible About Money.)
- Have you and your spouse walked the talk when it comes to money values?

RAISING CHILDREN TO BE
RESPONSIBLE ABOUT MONEY

We've all heard the horror stories of trust-fund babies gone wild and nanny-to-the-rescue reality shows. But take heart: Money doesn't necessarily spoil people and spoiled people don't necessarily have a lot of money. It's possible to raise responsible and productive children whatever your circumstances might be. Whether the young people in your life are your own, grandchildren, nieces and nephews, or godchildren, your financial walk and talk can have a substantial, positive impact on their relationship with money. It's never too late or too early to help them develop the skills they need to become fiscally responsible adults.

Your children's views about money are not created in a vacuum. Like it or not, you've been teaching them from the beginning. They've observed how you (and your spouse) talk about work, responsibility, and money for years. For instance, "Don't tell Mommy how much I really spent on our new computer setup." Or, "I know I would earn more doing something else, but I love teaching." They've also heard your actions speak louder than words. Add to this the incessant messages they are bombarded with every day from the media and peers about how cool they will be if they wear this or that sneaker and drink this or that soda, and you've got money-message overload. It's time for you to openly steer them where you want them to go.

Teaching your children about money presents an opportunity for you to improve your relationship with them and to help them grow. I've seen this play out beautifully over and over again when parents use the following approaches and tools.

First, some ways to help your children develop strong money values:

1. **Model what you want your children to imitate.** Take a look at your money walk and talk. Are you sending money messages that match your values? If not, change your talk and start walking a different path.

2. **Get on the same page as the other parent(s).** Talk with your children's other parent and stepparents, if any, about how to get into alignment. Consider a compromise, if necessary, to maintain consistency from parent to parent and household to household.

3. **Communicate honestly, not excessively.** Yes, communication is critical to raising responsible children. But children are, well, kids and not known for being discreet. Don't share any details that you wouldn't want the other carpool moms to know. I was in Connecticut one time and heard three schoolgirls talking about how much money their parents made. Not only were they playing a nasty game of one-upmanship, but they were also unthinkingly revealing private family information.

4. **Take the taboo out of money talk.** Make money a safe topic in your household. The more comfortable you are talking about money, the more comfortable your children will be, too. Use the tools below to help children learn money skills as early as possible, or come up with some of your own.

5. **Keep money in perspective.** Water relationships with the children in your life with time, attention, and fun—not just things. Money is only one aspect of life. Put it in its place as a tool, not an end in itself.

6. **Help children to develop an internal compass.** The best gift you can give children is an internal compass of values to guide them. Help them build a sense of integrity along with a belief in their own worth and ability to have a positive impact in the world. Focus on effort and improvement, not just a specific achievement.

7. **Provide money-earning opportunities early on.** Give your children plenty of chances to experience what it takes to earn a buck, both at home and away from home, as they get older.

8. **Encourage children to give something back.** Teach your children to give back to the family, community, and the

world with both time and money. Encourage them to be helpful without expecting compensation—whether shoveling the neighbor's snow for free when she has the flu or working a day in the local soup kitchen. From an early age, ask children to think about what causes are important to them and to donate even a small amount of whatever money they might have on a regular basis.

Now, some tools to help you along the way:

1. **Family Community Day.** Designate a certain day for the entire family to serve the community in some way—helping at a food bank, at a homeless shelter, in a nursing home, for a park cleanup, and so on. Let each child research and pick an organization, then draw straws to determine which cause to help first. Although many families do this during the holiday season, organizations often need the extra help even more during other times of the year.

2. **Big Adventure Bucks.** A personal favorite, I came up with this one for my own nieces and nephews. Many clients have loved using it with their families as well. For birthdays and holidays, consider giving Big Adventure Bucks instead of other presents. Make a certificate with the dollar amount and explain that when they turn 15 (at 16, driving is the only thing in mind!), they'll get to spend all the money on a big adventure that they research and choose, subject, of course, to parental approval. Along the way they will learn the benefits of saving and, as the money builds up, the various options for investing it until it's time to cash it in. This tool works well for families in all economic circumstances. For those with modest means, the money might add up to an evening watching the Knicks play basketball, whereas in a wealthier family the adventure might be a trip to the Yucatan during turtle hatching season.

3.   Family Investing Game. Consider having everyone in the family learn about the stock market, bonds, and funds by giving each member pretend, just-on-paper money. Every month, meet to see how the investments are doing and make adjustments. The adults can advise, but each person makes his or her own investing choices. At the end of the quarter or year, whomever earned the most money gets to pick the activity for a family outing. Then start over. This also provides you an opportunity to see what healthy or unhealthy competition exists between family members. By the time your children have real money to invest, they will have had enough experience to make sound decisions.

4.   Allowance. This age-old family tradition helps children learn about budgeting, saving, spending, and donating. There are two main camps of allowance philosophy—in payment for chores or independent of them—and each has its own merits. Some use a hybrid method of a guaranteed allowance with the opportunity to earn more for doing chores that go beyond the normal assignments. Encourage your children to open a bank account—and when old enough, a credit card— with their allowance so they will learn to balance their statements and gain experience dealing with financial institutions.

5.   Affirmation Books. The more children genuinely value themselves, the better they'll value everything and everyone around them. Affirmation books are an example of ways you can show children that their value doesn't lie in how much money they have or what possessions they own. Ask family, friends, teachers, and people the children look up to if they would write something they like about the particular child. Collect these statements into a beautiful binder and substitute it for another gift, such as the latest video game. Sure, older children might say these are hokey, but they will read the book and secretly cherish it.

Make the time to help the children in your life learn about money. Be intentional about how you go about it and use creative ways that will capture their attention. Give them the gift of a strong and positive start as they form their own relationship with money. And as you'll be reminded throughout this book, be sure to communicate, communicate, communicate!

- If your estate is sizeable, at what stage of life or maturity do you want your loved ones to have access to their inheritance?

5. Expectations and Assumptions

- Do your loved ones already have ideas or expectations about what they might receive or what roles they might play (that is, executor, guardian, and so on)?
- What do they think is going to happen with your estate?
- What does "equal" mean to you? What does it mean to your spouse? What does it mean to your children?
- What expectations might your children's spouses have?
- Are you assuming that your family knows what you would want to happen if you became incapacitated and unable to decide for yourself on matters related to finances or healthcare decisions?

6. What's Most Important?

- What do your loved ones *really* want from your estate?
- What do they think is missing from their life right now in terms of finances, possessions, career, relationship, and so on?
- What objects might your family fight over? What kinds of things or situations could potentially ruffle feathers?

- What traditions would your loved ones like to carry forward? What traditions would you like to see carried forward?
- Do you have particular causes or organizations you'd like to support?
- Is there anything that you want your family to know that they don't already know about you and what you think is important in life?
- What three things do you wish that someone had told you before their death?

Unless you are Superman or Superwoman, you probably won't be able to answer all of these questions without gathering some additional data. Start by simply thinking through them. Then begin to gather data passively, without letting everyone know what you are up to, to get the more honest and accurate read. When the subtle approach stops getting you what you need, don't hesitate to be more direct. (See sidebar: Signals It's Time to Talk.) You can find all sorts of communication tools and tips to guide you in Human Law Seven.

As you read through the rest of this book, answers to many of these questions will become more evident to you. You'll gain insight from seeing how other people address family dynamics during the will process—from appointing an executor to distributing your possesions, from formulating an equitable inheritance to using the will to make peace rather than to punish.

Now that you've begun to take an honest look at your family and considered their relationships, money values, and differing needs and expectations, it's time to take stock of all your stuff.

SIGNALS IT'S TIME TO TALK

Being subtle allows you to pick up information without putting your loved ones on the spot and can provide the most honest glimpse into what they are thinking. But sometimes being more direct is the only way to find out what you really need to know. Here are a few signs that it's probably time to bring things out into the open:

- Joking during Thanksgiving dinner about who is going to get what.

- Grade-school type gossip about how a sibling (or sibling's spouse) doesn't take good care of things, is stubborn, behaves rudely to their own kids, never visits, is snobby, and so on.

- Questions such as, "Hey, Mom. There are three of us and only one menorah. Who's going to get it?"

- No one in the family ever talks about money or what might happen when parents or grandparents die.

- No one in the family talks about anything else *except* what's going to happen when parents or grandparents die.

- Siblings and/or their families don't get along to the point of not speaking or spending any time together.

- Odd comments about money start slipping into conversations.

- Children ask questions about which side of the family is richer.

- Cousins say things to each other like, "Grandma bought me this new outfit! What, she didn't buy one for you? Guess she loves me more!"

- Intergenerational conversations are peppered with put-downs or slights such as, "You're getting so forgetful now, Mom, no wonder that happened."

- Sibling sniping shows up in the form of remarks like, "Suzanne's little Amy sure is fat, isn't she?" or, "Well, you know that Charlie always was a little pig-headed."
- Non sequiturs slip in at the end: "Thanks for dinner! We had such a good time. Guess we'll be getting home now. By the way, Dad, are you and Mom still using the RV anymore?"

Start with the Small Stuff, Then On to the Big Stuff

Judy was about to blow her lid. As she explained, "I'm not even in my grave and already my children are fighting over the cloisonné lamp that has been in the family for two generations." Judy's long-deceased mother had bought the exotic lamp with its enameled finish and elephant handles more than fifty years ago at an estate sale. It quickly became one of her mother's most loved and prized possessions. Perched on a stand next to her mother's bed for as long as Judy could remember, the lamp had served as a reading light. "In a strange way," Judy remarked, "it came to symbolize my mother's spirit—her zest for life, her unending curiosity, her nose always in a book. Now, whenever any of us see the lamp in my living room, Mother immediately comes to mind. It's taken on a life of its own."

According to two of Judy's children, Grandma Holland had promised each of them that they would get the lamp someday. Michael was adamant that as a teenager she had looked him straight in the eye and said, "This lamp will be yours one day." Sandy, on the other hand, claimed that on more than one occasion her grandmother had told her,

"One day you'll be married with your own home and this lamp will look beautiful in your living room." Since Thanksgiving, when the family had inadvertently stumbled upon the topic of Grandma Holland's lamp at the dinner table, Judy's two children had been incessantly feuding. As Judy concluded, "If this is any inkling of what's to come when I die, we're in big trouble."

Everyone has household contents and personal belongings that hold special meaning for them and their family members. These items run the gamut: photographs, quilts, special serving dishes, jewelry, rugs, cherished furniture, diaries and journals, awards and medals, yearbooks, artwork, and collections—coins, musical, literary, china, silver, stamps, and right down to the beloved box of holiday ornaments. While they may or may not have great financial worth—in fact, some of them might even be considered "junk"—what makes such items priceless is their emotional or sentimental value. As such, these possessions, which we refer to in this chapter as the "small stuff," can cause the most conflicts among family members, particularly during their time of grief. Full of memories, the small stuff is apt to cause or exasperate family rifts ranging from a hairline crack to the great divide. As well, how people feel about the way small stuff is handled can become a lightning rod for their overall feelings about the inheritance and the people with whom they share it. In legalese, the small stuff generally falls into the category called "tangible personal property." Ironically, these objects often become tangible reminders of who got what they wanted and who didn't. Long after the proceeds of your 401(k) have been divided up and forgotten, the small stuff still can be causing big damage to the relationships within your family.

Despite the importance of small stuff, people rarely

leave specific instructions in their wills about who gets the seemingly minor household or personal items. These emotionally charged possessions are given short shrift, or at best cursory treatment, in most plans for distributing the estate. Advisors typically ask you to jump right into the "big stuff"—things like your bank account, house, stock portfolio, insurance policy, and retirement savings. The fact is, even though the big stuff is more valuable, most of these assets are already liquid, or if not, can readily translate into cash. And cash is easily dividable. While $100,000 can be split into any number of portions after the sale of your home, how do you divide up a favorite painting received as a wedding present or an engagement ring? Testifying to the power of the small stuff, as one of my clients so aptly observed, "Let's face it. I am not going to fight my brother over which of us gets the Exxon stock versus the Chevron. Who cares? But when it comes to who ends up with Mom's blue Moroccan bowl, the one she served mashed potatoes in every Thanksgiving, you can bet I'm going to care!"

It's not that the big stuff isn't important. It certainly is. This chapter—which lays the groundwork for thinking about everything you have to leave including the larger assets—will definitely get to it. But first, let's take a look at the small stuff. What are the major considerations? How can you head off potential conflicts? What are some simple and manageable distribution solutions? Then we will turn our attention to the big stuff, from methods of inventorying what you have to whose name is on the title, from when you need to worry about taxes to what will go through probate. By the end of this chapter, you'll begin to see a much clearer picture of what you have so you can start to think about what you might want to do with it.

As you inventory and plan for distribution of your stuff—both big and small—the key point to remember is this: Ten years after you are gone you don't want anyone saying, "I'm still upset I didn't get the tin recipe box Mom bought at Woolworths in 1936." To prevent this from happening, keep thinking and asking yourself, "What will my loved ones really be fighting over?" Seven out of ten times, you can bet it will be over the small stuff. Spending a little time up front is the way to leave your family in peace, but doing so doesn't need to be a chore. In fact, my clients often find dealing with the small stuff one of the most satisfying parts of the estate distribution process. As I have heard from them time and time again, "Deciding how to pass along my treasures brought me a lot of joy."

Where We Stumble on the Small Stuff

Any reference to the small stuff usually shows up in statements like these, found in most standard boilerplate wills: "I leave my personal items and household contents to my children equally." Or, "To my children, I leave my personal effects and my tangible personal property in equal shares."

But what does "equal" really mean? Trying to answer this question is the first challenge when distributing the small stuff: Does it mean an equal number of items, equal dollar value, equal in terms of emotional worth, or some combination? Unfortunately, figuring out what equal means usually falls on the shoulders of the heirs themselves. Emotions already frayed, not only are they faced with going through mountains of memory-laden possessions, but they are also put in the awkward and uncomfortable position of figuring out the best way to divvy everything up among themselves. Unresolved feelings of parental favoritism, sibling rivalry, and animosity between in-laws, cousins, or the like can quickly rise to the surface as everyone jockeys for your personal possessions. Worse yet, some heirs ditch diplomacy altogether and engage in such free-for-all tactics like racing to a parent's home before the funeral to grab and haul off what they can before others arrive. Sad to say, this kind of behavior is actually more common than people realize. (See sidebar: Jackal Protection.)

When loved ones can't resolve distribution issues around the small stuff, then making decisions falls into the lap of the executor, who is usually left with nothing more than blind faith to rely on when deciphering your wishes. If the executor is one of your children, the task becomes even more difficult as he or she grapples with the dual role of managing the distribution and family relationships while juggling personal emotions and self interest. While arguments over the small stuff can border on the ridiculous—and even comical—to an outsider, they will escalate if not peacefully resolved. Sparks lit on the small stuff can quickly lead to wildfires. Do you really want an attorney mediating disputes over which child's claim to your fishing rod or stamp collection will stand? This happens all the time. The power of the small stuff is insidious, but as strong as the wind. If you don't watch out, it will blow seeds of division from one generation to the next.

JACKAL PROTECTION

Even when you've clearly stated your intentions for distributing household contents and personal possessions to loved ones or charity, it's always a good idea to have a jackal protection plan in place for securing your home upon death. This means asking a trusted friend, neighbor, or an executor to protect your home and its contents. Some counties have a public administrator who will come in and seal your house. If this does not automatically happen where you live, then ask a trusted friend or loved one to change the locks on doors and keep keys safely put away. This not only secures the home from loved ones until the will is read and possessions can be formally distributed according to your wishes, but it also protects against non-family members, such as housekeepers, neighbors, friends, and so on, who may have keys.

Another aspect of jackal protection is asking someone to baby-sit the house during funeral services since scavengers and thieves read the obituaries. Sometimes, especially with highly valuable estates or contentious circumstances, the executor will have someone stay in the house from death until distribution. Jackal protection is another good reason to keep an updated video of all items in your house so the executor and other family members know exactly what should be there. While none of this provides a guarantee that items won't be removed from your home, a jackal protection plan is better than having no system in place at all.

A jackal protection plan can also be invaluable if you become sick or otherwise incapacitated. Many of the tips mentioned above are equally useful if you need to be out of your house for an extended period due to illness or are employing caretakers in the home. Be prepared by instructing a friend or loved one to protect your belongings if the need should ever arise.

How Come Aunt Fran Stole
All the Expensive Stuff?

It was a seemingly innocent question, yet in one family it became the shot heard around the world. For many months, seven-year-old Courtney had been hearing conversations between her father and mother about estate-sharing conflicts they had been experiencing with her Aunt Fran. Last year, when Courtney's grandmother had died, her father said to his only sibling, "Look, Fran, I don't care about the stuff. Why don't you claim whatever you want and I'll just take the rest." Of course, it never occurred to him in his grief-stricken state that Fran might take everything of any monetary or emotional value, leaving only the crumbs behind. It also never occurred to him that while he was genuinely disinterested in his mother's possessions, his wife was *very* invested. And Fran, as Courtney's mother would later complain to anyone who would listen, "rushed in to take everything of any value, leaving our family to pick through the leftovers." Adding salt to the wound, Fran even billed the estate thousands of dollars in freight charges for shipping the items to her home in another state. Furious late-night conversations ensued between Courtney's parents about the shipping bill, which Courtney's father reluctantly had agreed to let the estate pay. That March, Aunt Fran invited little Courtney to come and spend a few days with her cousins during spring break. On the third night of her visit, she innocently asked her uncle in the middle of a dominos game, "How come Aunt Fran stole all the expensive stuff?" Aunt Fran was devastated when her husband relayed the incident to her. Word of little Courtney's question traveled fast to the extended relatives, quickly deepening the divide between brother and sister, cousin and cousin, in-law and in-law, husband and wife. In a dominos game that seems to have no end, Courtney has been ostracized by her cousins ever since and the two families rarely speak to each other to this day.

Considering the Small Stuff: Follow the Golden Rules

While people rarely have the time or energy to list each personal belonging, it's always best to identify the items most likely to cause commotion—be it for their emotional or financial value. So, before deciding how to divide up everything, first take stock of your small stuff by considering the following:

1. LOOK FOR THE HOT BUTTONS

Keeping family dynamics in mind throughout the estate planning process is a cornerstone of the Good Will approach. And when it comes to how family members get along after the will is read, the small stuff is usually the breeding ground for conflict. To give you an idea of the types of hot buttons to watch out for, here's a sampling of items the family members of my clients have fought over, fraying both nerves and relationships:

"Book of children's songs from 1911 that Dad sung us to sleep by."

"Grandma's weaving loom that came from Germany."

"Civil War diary handed down for generations."

"Losch hot-water boiler that just isn't made anymore."

"Mom's PTA service pin from the elementary school we all went to."

"Brass Sabbath candlesticks from Romania, the only memento of our family's pre-America days."

"Dad's varsity letters from college."

"Crokinole board game from our Canadian grandpa."

"Mom's famous purple journals where she wrote down practically everything that ever happened in the family."

"Grandma's engagement ring from 1921."

"The family piano that nobody plays and can't even be tuned anymore."

"The shovel Dad used to plant our garden that was made by a company that's no longer in business."

"China, not a whole china set, but the china bowl that Great Aunt Mattie painted on."

"The cradle that Granddad made from an old Ash tree in his backyard."

"Mom's cookbooks, especially the Betty Crocker one that's stained with food."

"A tractor that no longer works, but my dad and I used it together to work the land."

"The *Night Before Christmas* book that my parents read to each of us seven kids every holiday season."

"A Hanukkah tablecloth that my mother made in the 1950s with cut-out felt dreidels glued all over it."

"An old guitar that my father hadn't played for more than thirty years."

"The big, black cast-iron frying pan that Mom made our pancakes in every Sunday morning."

"My dad's old *Pogo* book—it was all torn, worn, and worth zilch."

The point is, everybody owns things that will press buttons. Usually there are a few items heirs immediately zone in on. For the Clausen children the immediate focus after their mother's death was on who got possession of the family's photo albums, their deceased father's World War II medals, an old and barely-working piano that had sat in the corner untouched for years, and an antique Hoosier cabinet their folks had brought with them from the Midwest. After that, the brothers made a beeline for the garage where they fought over the rusted hand tool collection and a canoe paddle inscribed with a wine list from the neighborhood restaurant their parents once owned. Similarly, the sisters grappled with who got their mother's cookbooks, a flea market china collection, and—most bizarre of all—an oversized and stuffed toy raccoon their mother had given their ailing grandmother in the hospital years ago.

2. ASK, LOOK BACK, AND RAISE YOUR ANTENNA GOING FORWARD

While most people think they know which belongings family members might be attached to and feud over, it's best to ask each loved one individually what is most important to him or her.

Just like with the stuffed raccoon, you might be in for a few surprises.

One family I recently worked with had a grandfather clock that the mother determined would go to her daughter and not her son who had never expressed an iota of interest in it. Soon after she made this decision, the son let on how hurt he was upon overhearing her talking about plans to leave the grandfather clock and other home furnishings to his sister. As Margaret recalled, "I couldn't believe my ears. My son is an avid outdoorsman who moves around a lot. Not for a second would I ever have thought he wanted that clock, much less any of the furniture." Because she could see what was on the horizon, Margaret was able to do something about her erroneous assumptions. She bought a small grandfather clock for her son and his wife at an estate sale as an anniversary present. They were touched by her thoughtfulness. As well, she talked to both children and found out which of her furnishings they each might want. Whatever you own, the earlier you start talking about the small stuff with your loved ones, the more time you will have to make things work out.

On the other hand, sometimes what you might think your loved ones want, they might not be interested in at all. Randy, a 65-year-old father, thought for sure that his son expected to inherit his entire book collection. Most of the books weren't rare, rather just hardcovers he had purchased from stores or book-of-the-month clubs and enjoyed reading over the years. But when Randy casually asked his son, also an avid reader, if he would like to have the books someday, only a few titles were of any interest to him. As Randy said, "Here I was saving a roomful of books to give to my son when he only wanted a handful." Two days after talking to his son, Randy donated most of his collection to the local library for its annual fundraising sale.

Inevitably, some people will find it too painful or uncomfortable to even broach these matters. If this describes you, at the very least reflect back on what your children have said in the past and keep your antenna raised for potential hot buttons as you go forward.

Pat and Phil, a couple in their 70s, had several children and grandchildren. When I inquired about their household furnishings, they said they didn't have much since they had recently moved to a smaller home. What items were left now, they wanted to specially designate to individuals in the family. Out of curiosity, I asked where the excess furnishings from the most recent downsizing had gone. They said primarily to one of their daughters, the only child who lived nearby, who had a spacious new home she was furnishing. I asked them whether that had ruffled any feathers with the other children. Pat thought for a minute, then said, "Well, about a year ago, I did call one of my other daughters who lives in Vermont. When we moved, I had given her one of my two favorite matching armchairs. I noticed on visits to her home that the armchair was just sitting in the garage. My daughter who lives nearby received the other chair in the set and was having a hard time matching it. So I called my daughter in Vermont and asked, since she wasn't using her chair, if she would let her sister have it." Pat was surprised to hear the answer, "Sure, I'll let her have it if she lets me take something in return from all that other stuff you already gave her." At the time, Pat thought that response was odd but brushed it off. Now upon reflection, she realized that perhaps there were some simmering tensions.

Pat asked me to speak to her daughter in Vermont, whose name is Lauren, to find out what was going on. When I called, her temper flared as she explained the "real" situation. When their parents downsized, Lauren's sister had agreed to store in her spacious basement the things that wouldn't fit into their new home—an arrangement that Pat seems to have forgotten about. Over time, many of the items had slowly moved from the downstairs to the upstairs of the sister's home. As Lauren said, "Every time I go to my sister's house for holidays we eat on the long table that once sat in my parents' dining room. I would have loved to have that! When my parents die, do you think she'll give it back to the estate? Fat chance. Every time I visit her, she's taken something else from my parents' stuff. On my last visit, I noticed a few choice items from my mother's china and silver collection gracing the dinner table as well. It's crazy, but all I can think about is my mom's engagement ring that was passed on from my grandmother who died decades ago. I bet you anything my sister is going to end up with that, too!"

Are there conflicts like this lurking just beneath the surface in your own family? Think, look back, and keep your antenna raised as you move forward. The feelings your loved ones express now about the small stuff are only a preview of conflicts to come.

3. DOUBLE CHECK THAT YOU OR YOUR SPOUSE HAVEN'T DOUBLE PROMISED

Complicating matters even more, when people do alert loved ones ahead of time, they sometimes make the mistake of double-promising. That is, more than one person has been told they can have the same item, like with Grandma Holland's cloisonné lamp.

Think back and catch yourself. Have you told more than one person that they can have something? Further, has your spouse or partner promised the very same object to another member of the family? Now is the time to get on the same page. I can't tell you how many times different people claim that one parent or grandparent promised them a special item, only to be overridden by the unknowing second parent. The story goes something like this. "My dad always said he wanted me to have his old music notebooks containing all the songs he wrote. After he died, my sister dropped off an envelope containing Xeroxes of the notebooks, saying that she was going to keep the originals because Mom was sure that Dad wanted them to go to her." Did the father really say that each of them should have the notebooks? Perhaps. Or it could simply be an honest error, that is, the wife believed her husband had wanted one thing, when he had already promised something else. Ask yourself and your spouse or partner, "What have we already told people about who gets this item?" If you find you've made double promises, correct them now to prevent disappointment and conflict down the road.

4. RECOGNIZE WHEN OTHER FACTORS MIGHT BE IN PLAY

If you've asked and find that two or more people want the same item, take a step back as a parent or giver, and ask whether there is another issue involved. If so, addressing *that* will keep the peace. Sometimes children aren't really interested in the item itself, rather just owning a stronger connection to you. For example, if your daughter is making a fuss over your giving a baseball from the World Series to your son, even though she has no interest in baseball, is she actually calling out for something else? How can you take the emotional charge out of the item? While parents often try to substitute something else in situations like these by giving them a "make-up item," you should recognize that feelings may have nothing to do with the item itself. Sometimes the best solution is to build a stronger connection with your loved one. Ask yourself, "How can I show that I love them? How can I give them more attention now? How can I help them feel worthy?" How they'll end up feeling about whatever you leave them all goes back to whether the inheritance stirs the pot of insecurity and fear or reflects your love and care.

5. USE THE SMALL STUFF AS BARGAINING CHIPS

Most people underestimate the power of the small stuff in the larger estate distribution context—particularly in the case of an unequal inheritance—in helping to even the score or prevent hard feelings. While we will give examples of this in later chapters, it's important to recognize that personal possessions—along with a heartfelt letter explaining their significance—can go a long way toward healing hearts and making loved ones embrace your final wishes.

6. DO THE BEST YOU CAN

When it comes to the small stuff, it's impossible to head off every potential conflict and know how your decisions are going to affect your loved ones. Issues about the small stuff often have little to do with the parent. Sometimes it's more about sibling relations, such as sharing issues that were never resolved while growing up or age-old rivalries rising to the surface after years of lying dormant. Your will might stir up old insecurities and magnify past problems or miscommunication. As one man commented over his brother getting something from his mother's estate that he wanted, "It's sad to say, but my brother was always the football star in school growing up and got all the attention. And now, thirty years later, he comes out on top once again." However imperfect or challenging distributing the small stuff is, taking the onus off your kids is one of the greatest gifts you can pass on. Otherwise, you leave the door wide open for them to duke it out in their time of grief.

Methods for Distributing the Small Stuff

You can decide ahead of time who gets what. Or, instead of predetermining where you want each of your possessions to go, you can formally state a distribution method to be used after you are gone. What you *don't* want to do is leave the details of distribution to grieving loved ones— which is exactly what happens with vague, boilerplate language that says something like, "All personal items and household contents pass on to my children equally."

Whatever way you go, you'll need to decide whether to announce your plan to the heirs now or wait for them to find out after you're gone. Whether now or later, the more reasons you give for your decisions, the better. Most children will be hard pressed not to respect your wishes if they are thoughtfully explained. By expressing them, you avert potential bitterness among loved ones and build bridges to future family peace.

Bear in mind that no one system is perfect or right for every family. Make sure to first identify your goals and address them with your course of action. Like a buffet, you can pick and choose from among the various distribution methods. One way might work well for certain items, while another choice might be best for others. Additionally, one approach could be perfect at this point in your family's life, whereas later another method or combination might work better. From time to time, be sure to reevaluate your plan and determine if it still makes sense given current circumstances.

Let me take you through the different approaches and trade-offs for each.

1. DECIDE WHO GETS WHAT WHILE YOU ARE STILL HERE.

There are several options you can consider when it comes to clearly expressing your desires for each unique item of personal property before you go.

Give It Away While You're Still Alive.　Simply identify the items and distribute them to your loved ones ahead of time. You could do this over a period of time and deal with each of your heirs individually, or you could gather the family together to thoughtfully distribute your significant possessions all at once. Sometimes people use gifting during life as a way to reduce the potential for estate tax after death. But if you have unusually expensive items that you plan to give away, be careful not to exceed the gift tax limits. Consult an attorney for advice if you think that the value of the items you are planning to gift will be greater than $11,000 per person in a given year. Note that you and your spouse can *each* give $11,000. This means, for example, that if you and your spouse pass on items to a son and his wife, the total value for a given year should not exceed $44,000. Naturally there will be possessions you won't want to part with until after you leave the planet. For example, your wedding and engagement rings or furniture still in service. For these items, simply designate their intended recipients or use one of the other methods mentioned below.

Leave Detailed Instructions in Your Will. Make an itemized list in your will of your household contents and personal belongings stating to whom you wish each item to go. You could also just focus on the key items of emotional and financial value with the rest to be distributed using a second method. The drawback of using your will as the place to declare your wishes concerning the small stuff is needing to continually update it as circumstances change. As well, the contents of your will become public record following your death.

Prepare a Side Letter, Photo Journal, or Video. To avoid the need to constantly update the will and to maintain confidentiality, people often use some other means of stating their wishes that they then refer to in their will. While, as mentioned earlier, loved ones will be hard-pressed not to respect your wishes if they are thoughtfully expressed, be aware that not all states recognize other forms—such as referenced lists, letters, photo journals, or videos—as legally binding, even when attached to the will. To find out what will work in your state, consult with an attorney. You can write a letter—even in your own handwriting— that expresses your wishes and attach it to your will. In lieu of a written list, walk around your home and photograph or videotape selected personal possessions and designate to whom they should go. In the case of a photograph, state the name of the intended recipient on the back of each photo or place all the photos in an album with the name of the person next to each photo. Whatever the case, leave the photo journal or videotape in the same place as you keep your will and make sure it's clearly labeled. The more people you tell about its existence, the better.

Tag It.   Sometimes people write directly on the underside or backside of an article or affix a label to the item stating the name of the person to whom they want it to go. A word of caution with this method: While it might sound easier to do, it's also easy for heirs to mess with the tags or for them to even fall off. Take your own family dynamics into consideration when using this approach. It's often most useful for certain possessions, rather than an entire household of stuff. One woman who found this method particularly helpful had a passion for prints that she had collected at tag sales and antique shops throughout her life. After walking around her house to decide who would get what, she wrote a personal note to accompany each print. She put the note in an envelope, which she then affixed to the back of the picture frame. For example, to her firstborn son she wrote:

Dear Jordan,
 I bought this print framed at an antique shop in Great Barrington on my 42nd birthday. I wanted to buy something special for myself and saw this, which reminded me of my early days of motherhood and all the cherished moments I had with you when you were a baby. Now as I write this, you are already ten years old! Someday, when I am long gone, I hope this print will find a special place in your home and in your heart.

Love,
Mom

2. IF YOU DON'T DECIDE AHEAD OF TIME, THEN FORMALLY PRE-STATE A METHOD OF DISTRIBUTION FOR DIVIDING UP YOUR HOUSEHOLD CONTENTS AND PERSONAL BELONGINGS.

If you don't decide who gets what before you go, then at least state how you want your heirs to divide up the small stuff so that in the middle of their grief that don't have to figure it out themselves. Here are a few methods to choose from that you can state either in your will, living trust, or a side letter.

Use Rotating Choice. This method essentially allows heirs to take turns in choosing the items they want. One of the first steps is to decide what order people will go in. You can pre-state a system to use, be it by the flip of a coin, drawing straws or cards, choosing names out of a hat, and so on. Some people choose who goes first on the basis of birth order, but keep in mind that the more random the system, like drawing straws, the less potential for hard feelings. At the end of this process, anything that is left is sold in a garage or estate sale with proceeds split among heirs, donated to charity, or hauled to the dump.

You might consider another means for dividing up big-ticket items or those with the most emotional punch by taking them out of the running. Either specifically name who should get each of these, or consider holding a second rotating choice session just for them. Frequently the excluded items are simply those with a lot of the same thing, such as original photographs or collections of any sort. People often find holding separate rotating choice rounds for that category results in a fairer distribution system for everyone involved.

Add Dollar Value to the Rotating Choice Method. A pure rotating choice method is largely based on the luck of the draw and might result in one "greedier" sibling walking away with the most expensive items or making people feel torn between picking possessions with the most financial value versus that with the most sentimental value. To avoid this, some families will assign a dollar value to each item prior to holding the rotating choice session. The total amount of the items chosen by each heir is then deducted from his or her portion of the estate. Since ultimately the money value gets balanced out in the end, people feel less obligated to choose the more expensive possessions but rather use their turns to acquire the items that have the most meaning for them. In valuing the items, some families will call in a formal appraiser for expensive property, ask a person who specializes in tag sales or flea markets for an informal appraisal, or simply get together with other family members to make a monetary appraisal of each item themselves.

Although considering financial value of items in a rotating choice system works well for many families, it still doesn't address the emotional value that can't readily be translated into a dollar amount. That's why some people request that their loved ones use the rotating choice process, but elect to let the chips fall where they will. If one child wants to spend a turn to get Dad's pipe because of the memories it provides and skips picking something worth hundreds of dollars, then who can say which item is really of more value to the members of that family?

Take a Tour, Tag, and Let Lady Luck Decide. In this method, you simply specify that family members go around your home and put their name on things. For those items on which two or more names appear, flip a coin or draw straws to determine who gets it. In this case you could also use the option of assigning a dollar value to each item and deducting it from that person's portion of the estate.

3. IF YOU DON'T THINK YOUR FAMILY CAN HANDLE THE SMALL STUFF PEACEFULLY USING ANY OF THESE METHODS, THEN CONSIDER AN AUCTION OR TAG SALE.

If you believe that your children won't be able to handle matters peaceably no matter what, the last option is simply stating in your will that all your household contents and personal belongings are to be sold at a public or family auction—or tag sale—with the proceeds to be split equally among heirs.

That was the case of one Texas family. The parents had five children from two marriages and sixteen grandchildren. When they downsized, moving from the family home to a smaller condo in a retirement community, they got a preview of what might happen after they died. As the family patriarch commented, it was "guerilla warfare over paintings, chairs, tables, tools, the lawn mower, even extra pots and pans." In their will, instead of making a list of who got what, they indicated that they wanted everything sold at a private family auction. Each family member would be entitled to bid on any object with the winning amounts deducted from that person's share of the estate. Anything left over was directed to be donated to charity.

4. SOME ITEMS MERIT SPECIAL CONSIDERATION: GIFTS, PHOTOS, COLLECTIONS, SPECIAL JEWELRY, AND TREASURED FURNISHINGS.

Whatever overall system you choose, you can always exempt certain items. There are usually some possessions that merit special distribution instructions. The ones that are most often handled separately include gifts from loved ones, photos, collections of any sort, special jewelry, and treasured furnishings.

Gifts.   Allow loved ones to take back anything in your estate that they gave you. So, for example, daughter Susan gets back the fine ceramic plates that she had bought her mother in Turkey on her summer vacation there. Her brother gets back all the Christmas caroler figurines that he and his wife had given his mother over the past twenty years. Be aware, however, that people have short memories. You might want to remind people in writing who gave you what and require that they flip a coin to determine where the item goes in case of an irresolvable dispute.

Photos.   The same holds true with original photographs—particularly baby and school photos. Consider returning any photo of an heir to that person. If you are using a rotating choice system, consider running a separate round just for photos. You might include the requirement that whoever gets an original is, at the estate's expense, obligated to provide copies to anyone who wants them. Another issue that frequently comes up is breaking up family photo albums since children often want to leave them intact. One creative solution I've heard about is a shared custody approach. Three siblings decided to take turns hosting a treasured family album—carefully assembled by their mother over many decades—in one-year rotating intervals. That way they can each enjoy sharing the album with their own families without dismantling their mother's labor of love.

Collections.   Collections are often viewed under state law as one item. When considering collections, be specific. For example, don't indicate that you are leaving your silver to Julie if you don't mean every piece of silver in your entire house. Or, if you have a stamp collection, you would probably not want the entire collection to be considered one item for a rotating choice distribution process.

Special Jewelry.   When it comes to important pieces of jewelry—most notably a wedding or engagement ring—get creative. Recently over lunch, one of my friends shared that just before her grandmother died, she wisely had her diamond wedding ring taken apart, leaving a gem to each of the females in the family to have set as they wished as a necklace or ring.

Treasured Furnishings.   Most families have a few one-of-a-kind items that are considered special by everyone—such as the dining room hutch, a rocking chair from Grandma's farm, or a handmade cradle. You can either let chance take care of it by leaving these items in a general distribution system, or separate them out and specify which goes to whom.

A Final Thought on the Small Stuff

"I'm getting rid of all my junk."

Jenny was concerned about her next-door neighbor and dear friend Alice, a 42-year-old homemaker. A few weeks ago, Alice lost her father, her last surviving parent. As executor of his estate, she had been spending every waking hour since the funeral going through her father's home, figuring out who gets what among her out-of-town siblings, and planning a neighborhood tag sale for unloading the leftovers. Just the other day, Alice had met with several Realtors to discuss putting her father's home on the market. Alice was exhausted.

Looking out her window late at night, Jenny was surprised to see all the lights still ablaze next door. Earlier in the day, she had noticed Alice furiously moving things from house to garage. Jenny was concerned, so she wandered across the lawn and knocked on her neighbor's front door. When Alice appeared, Jenny asked what was keeping her so busy into the wee hours. Alice replied dryly, "I'm getting rid of all my junk."

Anyone who has been through the process of emptying out someone else's house following a death or during a serious illness knows exactly what Alice was talking about. Not only is it emotionally draining to go through a beloved family member's possessions, but the sheer volume of it can be physically overwhelming.

Spending all of those days clearing out her father's home had compelled Alice to think about how much junk was stuffed in her own. As Alice later noted to Jenny with a lighthearted chuckle, "I wouldn't want to leave this job to my worst enemy."

Do you really want the children wading through your collection of three hundred ancient *National Geographic* or *Life* magazines? The stuffed pheasant bagged on a hunting trip that sits in the attic and makes your grandchildren wince? Everything else you've acquired over the years but no longer use—from the fad exercise machine to the broken-down lawn mower you never got around to fixing?

You're never too young to start thinking about letting go of your excess of possessions. One client of mine, a wonderful woman, died at age 39 leaving behind her husband and two young children. Once she became ill, no one had time to think about all of her things stored in the garage—everything from boxes of papers written in college to half-finished sewing projects to furniture bought at estate sales with plans to restore someday. Two years after her death, everything still sits in the garage. Her husband simply can't bear the pain of going through it all.

The more organized and less cluttered your life, the easier it's going to be on your family when you go—whenever that might be. Save them the hassle, as well as the emotional and physical turmoil, by beginning to sort through your small stuff now. Consider clearing out and distributing unneeded possessions along the way as you enter new stages in life. Whatever you do, don't wait until it's too late.

On to the Big Stuff

Do you have a house, a retirement account, an insurance policy, a bank account, or a car? This is the "big stuff" when it comes to what you have to leave your loved ones. But before you try to decide who gets what, first take the time to identify all of your assets and liabilities as of today. At the end of this chapter you will find my *What You Have to Give Inventory* which identifies the information you'll need when consulting with lawyers, attorneys, or other estate advisors—and especially when going the do-it-yourself route. *The What You Have to Give Inventory* will prompt you to note significant details including type of ownership, current value, purchase price, location of records, and other relevant facts for each category of assets. Taking the time to carefully gather this data now will likely save you both time and frustration down the road. Knowing detailed information up front about what you own and what you owe will make it far easier to determine who you want to get what.

The following discussion will be more meaningful if you take a moment to eyeball the *What You Have to Give Inventory* at the end of this chapter. You can also download the inventory at www.creatingthegoodwill.com. Now, let's walk through the terms you'll encounter when using the inventory, including various types of property, different forms of ownership, and other aspects of your assets. Along the way, I'll address the often confusing issues of estate tax and probate. So hang on, this section has a lot for you to digest! Feel free to skip or skim through the parts that don't apply to your situation and focus on the aspects that seem most relevant.

TYPES OF PROPERTY

For legal purposes, property is generally classified in the following three ways:

1. Real property. Homes, land, buildings, condominiums, and other things that cannot be moved.

2. Tangible personal property. Things you can see, touch, and move. In addition to the small stuff we discussed earlier in the chapter, this also includes big-ticket items like cars, boats, livestock, farm machinery, and so on.

3. Intangible personal property. Papers that represent items you own such as bonds, stocks, mutual funds, bank accounts, retirement accounts, life insurance policies, and future interests. Future interests include any funds or property that you might receive in the future. For example, you are named in a trust but don't yet have access to its contents. Owning an insurance policy on another person is also a future interest that you can leave to someone else. Certain types of intangible personal property, including life insurance, annuities, and retirement accounts, allow you to name beneficiaries directly in the property contracts themselves or in special forms rather than in your will.

FORMS OF OWNERSHIP

It's not only important what you own, but also how you own it. The form of ownership for a given piece of property governs how you can transfer it—both now and upon death—and can also have tax implications. Not all states recognize the same forms of ownership. Do you know how you hold title to your house, car, and bank accounts? Look at your deed, title, or financial statements to find out. If you have any uncertainty or questions about how you own specific assets, consult with an attorney or accountant to confirm the current status. Ask whether other ownership options might make more sense, given the state you live in and your circumstances. Here are descriptions of six major forms of ownership:

1. Sole Ownership.   One person owns all interest in an item of property and has full control over keeping it, selling it, and giving it away.

2. Joint Tenancy with Rights of Survivorship.   Two or more people own something together, most often real estate. When one joint tenant dies, the remaining parties continue to own the property in equal shares. So if two people own the property, the survivor gains 100 percent ownership when the other person dies. If there are three joint tenants involved, each of the other two survivors will have one-half ownership when the third dies. A survivor's right to own is called right of survivorship. Many couples own their home as joint tenants with the right of survivorship to keep it out of probate. Cheap and easy to create, joint tenancy avoids probate, protects property from the creditors of a deceased joint tenant, and makes assets available to the surviving joint tenant(s) immediately after your death. However, joint tenancy can cause problems in cases of divorce or remarriage, doesn't protect against one joint tenant taking action without permission of the other owner(s), can be subject to gift and estate taxes unless the joint tenant is a spouse, and eliminates the ownership rights of a surviving spouse who is not part of the joint tenancy arrangement.

3. Tenancy in Common.   Two or more people, each called a tenant in common, own a share in the same property at the same time without the right of survivorship. The shares are not necessarily equal and do not automatically go to a spouse upon death.

4. Tenancy by Entirety.   This is a form of joint tenancy that is available to married couples in certain states and provides protection against the creditors of a spouse. The approval of both spouses is required before a property can be mortgaged or sold. Because this is a joint tenancy, there is a right of survivorship. The surviving spouse automatically becomes the sole owner of the property. In some states Tenancy by Entirety only applies to real estate. Complications can arise if one spouse becomes incapacitated without making someone their agent to make financial decisions.

5. Community Property.   This special form of ownership for married couples is recognized by the following nine states: Arizona, California, Idaho, Louisiana, Nevada, New Mexico, Texas, Washington, and Wisconsin. In these states, property that you alone owned prior to marriage continues to be your sole property after marriage. Personal gifts and inheritances obtained after marriage are also considered the sole property of the person receiving them. Each spouse, however, is entitled to an equal 50 percent interest in any property acquired during the marriage. Alaska allows couples to opt in for community property ownership.

6. Life Estate.   Also called a life tenancy, this gives someone the right to use the property during his or her lifetime after which it goes to someone else who is called a remainderman.

OTHER ASPECTS OF YOUR ASSETS

How and when property will be transferred.   Property can be distributed to your loved ones during your lifetime, upon your death, and/or after certain conditions of a trust are met. You can transfer assets according to instructions in your will, through joint ownership, by giving them as gifts, by selling them (according to the laws of the state when there's no will), and on beneficiary forms for certain items such as retirement accounts or insurance policies. When leaving assets to a minor, you should appoint someone to oversee the inheritance until the child turns at least 18.

Asset value.   What is the asset worth now and what did you pay for it? By stating the original purchase price, you will make it easy on your executor and/or attorney who may need to establish the tax basis of the property to determine potential tax obligations. Additionally, this information can help you to determine the potential tax advantages of giving one asset over another when making charitable donations. For insurance policies, call your broker to find the current cash value, if any.

Asset description.   Clearly identify the asset by stating the location of real estate, the model number/year of vehicles, account or loan numbers for intangible property, and so on.

Location of records and documents.   Make it easy for your executor by telling him or her where to find the paperwork associated with each asset and the contact information of any person who might have additional information, such as your banker or broker. Be sure to mention where the following can be found: mortgage and title papers for your home, credit card and bank account information, beneficiary forms from insurance policies or retirement plans, contracts related to loans or rents due to you, and even statements from your frequent flyer programs. In addition to information about your assets and property, be sure to let the executor know where to find safety deposit and post office boxes, keys, and combinations; adoption documents; divorce papers; social security card; birth and marriage certificates; documents for funeral prearrangements; computer passwords; an inventory of your safety deposit box; warranty materials; and access codes for home, office, auto, garage door, and bank accounts.

Money owed to you.   Be sure to determine anything that is owed to you from the rental income on a property you own to an informal loan you've made to a loved one. If you have any informal loan arrangements, this is the time to be sure to have something in writing, especially if the person is also going to be inheriting from your estate. If you decide to forgive the loan, be sure to consider the impact of this decision on other loved ones.

Beware, however, that if you forgive a significant loan or make one without a formal agreement, it can be considered to be a gift for tax purposes. If the gifts given in a year are less than $11,000 per person—or up to $44,000 when the money is from you and your spouse and given to another couple such as your son and his wife—then no problem. But say you loaned your daughter $50,000 that she never paid back; you will have made a taxable gift and might be liable for a 55 percent gift tax on the amount plus interest. In these situations, be sure to consult an attorney or accountant for advice.

What's All the Fuss About Taxes?

When property passes from the deceased to the heirs, the federal and state governments are entitled to tax the inherited property with federal estate tax and the state death tax. In many states your estate will not owe state death tax unless it is first determined to owe federal estate tax. Your estate does not pay tax on things you leave your spouse. Instead, these assets if still owned will face estate tax when he or she dies. Property you leave to charity is also tax exempt. Keep in mind that what you've already given as gifts are no longer owned by you and are not part of your estate. Gifts have their own set of separate tax rules and can face a gift tax rate of up to 55 percent when the gift is made. However, gifts are only taxable if in any one calendar year you give more than the allowable amount, which is called the annual exclusion. In any calendar year an individual can give up to $11,000 each to any number of people or trusts—double that for gifts from a married couple. Many people use this exclusion to reduce the value of their estate. The value of any taxable gifts you have made can either be taxed the year in which they were made or applied to reduce the estate tax exemption in effect the year of your death.

Historically, no estate tax was charged on an individual's estate valued at less than $1,000,000. Under the Revenue Act of 2001, and unless the laws change again in the meantime, the tax-free exemption will be $2,000,000 for 2006–2008 and $3,500,000 for 2009. If you are really worried about your heirs paying estate tax, then you might want to know that none will be charged at all for those who die in 2010. Try to figure that one out!

In the past, estate tax rates ranged from 18 percent to 55 percent (ouch). However, the new 2001 laws bring down the maximum rate to 47 percent for 2006, 46 percent for 2007, and 45 percent in 2008–2009. In 2010, it drops to 0 percent and then rises back to 50 percent in 2011, again all unless the law changes. Many experts expect a change soon.

The Gross Estate

The total amount of what is called your gross estate determines whether or not estate taxes will be due and, if so, how much will be owed. The gross estate is used only for tax purposes and is calculated by adding up the value of particular types of assets that you leave, then deducting certain exclusions including marital property and specific expenditures. Items that are part of the gross estate may or may not go through the probate process (see the following section). You can find helpful tips on how to calculate your estate tax liability at the IRS website www.IRS.gov. If you think your estate might be subject to taxes, be sure to consult with an attorney and/or an accountant.

- **Solely owned property.** Anything that was individually owned by the deceased—whether 100 percent of something or an undivided part—is included in the gross estate.

- **Certain gifts made within three years of death.** Here the IRS tries to recapture assets that may have been given away at the last minute to avoid being taxed. A good example is a life insurance policy that was owned by my client on her own life. In this case, she gave away the policy four years ago prior to her death. The IRS then checked to find out if the proper gift tax was paid or if the policy was purchased by someone at market value. Note that as long as you are alive, even if you become incapacitated, you can still use the annual exclusion to make gifts to individuals and trusts provided that you have first given someone a power of attorney to do so.

- **Survivor annuity or pensions.** If your spouse has already passed away and you receive money from certain kinds of pensions or annuities, whatever remains in the accounts after your death is included in your gross estate.

- **Trust assets under certain circumstances.** If it's determined by the IRS that the deceased person retained too much control over assets placed in certain kinds of irrevocable trusts, the value of the trust can be pulled back into the gross estate. A living trust can be revoked at any time and so, although it won't be subject to the probate process, it's value *is* included in the owner's estate with some exceptions. This is a perfect example of why it makes sense to consult attorneys when setting up trusts.

- **Jointly owned property.** If a joint tenant is your spouse, half of the value of the jointly owned property will be included for tax purposes in each spouse's estate. If the joint tenants are not married, the tax liability depends on a number of factors, so it's best to consult with an accountant or attorney.

- **Life insurance proceeds.** When the deceased owned the policy on him- or herself—regardless of whether the beneficiary is the estate or a named individual—the proceeds are part of the gross estate. You could have multiple policies naming different people as beneficiaries. Your insurance might have cash value or be a term policy that only offers benefits upon death. For estate tax purposes, it doesn't matter. Who owns the policy is the determining factor for the taxability of an insurance policy.

- **Life insurance cash value.** If the deceased owned a life insurance policy on someone else's life, the cash value (if any) of that policy becomes part of the gross estate.

Items deducted from the gross estate before taxes are calculated:

- **Marital property.** All property that goes to a surviving spouse outright or through certain qualified marital trusts. These items might be taxed when the surviving spouse dies.

- **Charitable donations.** All property donated in the will to a tax-exempt charity is taken out of the gross estate.

- **Estate expenses.** Probate filing fees, executor fees, attorney fees, funeral expenses, and debts on estate property—mortgages, unpaid bills and taxes, funeral expenses, and so on.

- **Certain percent of any state death tax paid.** This depends on the state you live in.

Untangling the Probate Process

Probate is the cumbersome system states use to determine who gets what when someone dies. Generally considered to be an antiquated process, probate creates a set of legal hoops the estate must jump through before its contents can be distributed. Primarily a clerical and administrative function that involves a thick pile of documents that must be filled out and filed, probate can take from several months to several years to complete. The contents of a will become public information once they go through the probate process. Using a living trust as the primary vehicle for communicating who gets what allows those assets to stay out of probate (while still subject to estate tax) and protects confidentiality about the heirs and the value of what they inherited. The will still goes through probate, but it simply references the trust without listing the specifics of what's in it. Because the assets in the living trust don't go through probate, they can be more quickly distributed.

During probate contents of the estate are inventoried and appraised, creditors and taxes are paid, and the court reviews the will to "prove" (the source of the word "probate") that it's valid. Unless the will is contested, many states will complete the process without a formal hearing. Finally, if any goodies are left, they will be distributed according to the will and other legally recognized estate documents. If you don't have a will when you die, the state will decide what to do with everything you have according to its own laws.

Probate fans (few and far between, probably a handful of attorneys) claim probate prevents fraudulent transfer of the decedent's property and protects beneficiaries by limiting the time creditors have to claim payment from the estate. While we do need a process to facilitate wills, we most certainly could improve on how probate currently works. Many states are actively looking into doing just that.

One of the major complaints against probate is its cost. An AARP report claims that probate attorneys annually receive fees of $1.5 billion. As with executors, in many states probate attorney fees are whatever the court approves as reasonable. Recently in New York, $1,600 per hour was deemed reasonable for work done on a complex case. For typical situations, expect that probate can cost up to 10 percent of the estate assets, including attorney fees, filing fees, and executor fees. Some states simply allow a percentage of the estate value to be spent on legal fees related to probate. Add court costs, appraisals, and any extra fees charged by the attorneys for "extraordinary" services rendered and it's easy to see how a significant chunk of even a modest estate can get eaten up in probate.

So, is an attorney really necessary for probate? States such as California and Wisconsin have established procedures that allow executors to walk through the probate process without an attorney. Going it alone is not impossible elsewhere, but I don't recommend it. Often there are obscure details and very specific ways probate documents must be written that are difficult to adhere to without an attorney. Also, any little mistake can hold up the process and quite frankly, annoy the court clerks and judges making it all take even longer. If cost is a concern, executors of modest and uncomplicated estates might be able to obtain better rates if they negotiate for them in advance. They can ask the attorney to quote a fixed fee for handling probate. Get it in writing though, and have it signed.

What goes through probate?

- The will itself, even if it leaves everything to a trust.
- All property held in the deceased person's name alone.
- All property passing to a spouse through the will.
- Co-owned property when the share owned by the deceased does not automatically pass to other co-owners, such as property held as a tenant in common.
- Partnership interests.
- Interests in corporations.
- The deceased spouse's share of community marital property in one of the community property states (see Forms of Ownership above).
- Life insurance policy owned by the deceased and payable to the estate rather than an individual or an institution. Note: Don't ever let this be your situation!
- Life insurance policy owned by the deceased on someone else's life.
- Certain gifts made within three years of passing.

What is exempt from probate?

- Many states provide greatly simplified procedures for modest estates, for example, those under $3,000 in Alabama and those under $100,000 in certain situations in California.
- In most states, property passing from one spouse to the other if owned as joint tenants.
- Property owned jointly with right of survivorship.
- Anything that is placed in certain types of trusts including a living trust.
- Assets with a named beneficiary including life insurance, retirement accounts, pensions, and annuities. Although

each account or policy will have its own rules, you generally use a special "Beneficiary Designation Form" to name the person or people you wish to receive these assets.

- Pay-on-death accounts. You can set up a bank account (and some types of government bonds) that will be paid out to a specific person upon your death. Other types of pay-on-death arrangements exist on a state-by-state basis. For example, in Missouri and California, you are allowed to transfer your car this way.

What You Have to Give

The following inventory is simply a way for you to identify all of your assets and liabilities at this moment in time along with some important information specific to the type of asset or liability. For example, you might want to leave your home to your three children, but first you need to ask yourself what type of ownership it's under, what it's worth, how much you still own on it, and so on. Don't forget to update your information periodically—many people make this part of their New Year's routine.

Before making an appointment with the attorney or attacking that will on your own, clean out file drawers, dig up old accordion folders, and go through those stacks of statements on your desk. Get a grip on what you've got to give when it comes to the big stuff and let your inventory be a guide as you start to create the Good Will.

Now that you've taken stock of your stuff, large and small, and before you make any final decisions on what you want to do with it, it's time to think about putting your team in place.

What You Have to Give Inventory

I. ASSETS

Liquid Assets	Financial Institution	Account Number	Who Owns It (How Titled)
Cash			
Savings Account(s)			
Checking Account(s)			
Money Market Account(s)			
Certificates of Deposit			
Private Annuities			

Stocks, Bonds, Mutual Funds, Etc.	Description	Identifying Information	Who Owns It (How Titled)
Government Bonds			
Corporate Bonds			
Mutual Funds			
Tradable Stocks and Securities			

Retirement Benefits	Type of Plan	Identifying Information	Owner
Vested interest in 401(k), Profit Sharing, Pension, Keogh, IRAs, etc.			
Death Benefits			

Life Insurance Policies	Insurance Company	Policy Number	Owner
Policy You Own on Your Life			
Policy You Own on Someone Else's Life			

Frequent Flyer Miles/ Credit Card Bonus Points	Description	Member Number	Member Name on Card
Airline			
Card Company			

Real Estate	Description of Property	Mortgage Information	Who Owns It (How Titled)
Residence			
Other Land			
Second Home			
Condominium			
Fee Simple Timeshare Interest			
Business Property (if sole proprietorship)			

Contact Info.	Location of Records	Purchase Price	Value Today

Contact Info.	Location of Records	Purchase Price	Value Today

Contact Info.	Location of Records		Value Today

Contact Info.	Location of Records	Death Benefit Amount	Cash Value Today

Contact Info.	Location of Records	Points Accumulated	Dollar Value

Contact Info.	Location of Records	Purchase Price	Value Today

Business Personal Property	Description	Identifying Information	Who Owns It (How Titled)
Patents, Copyrights, Royalties, Trademarks			
Interests in Partnership, LLC, LLP, Closely-Held Corporation (family business, farm, ranch, etc.)			
Long-term Leases (including timeshares if not fee simple timeshares)			
Sole Proprietorship Business and Property (equipment, inventory, improvements, etc.)			
Miscellaneous—Loans, Mortgages, Rents, Professional Service Fees, etc., Owed to You			

Other Personal Property	Description	Loan Information	Who Owns It (How Titled)
Precious Metals			
Valuable Household Goods (rugs, furniture, art, silver, china, etc.)			
Jewelry and Furs			
Collections			
Musical Instruments			
Sporting Equipment			
Tools/Equipment			
Livestock/Animals			
Personal Loans Owed to You			
High-Ticket Technology (computers, etc.)			
Co-op Apartments			
Vehicles, Cars, Boats, Motorcycles, etc.			

Other Assets	Type of Asset	Identifying Information	Who Owns It (How Titled)
Future Interests You Expect to Receive			
Trust Distributions			

Contact	Location of Records	Purchase Price/ Cost Basis (what you paid/ earned/contributed for your interest)	Value of Your Interest Today

Contact Info.	Location of Records	Purchase Price	Value Today

Contact Info.	Location of Records		Value Today

It's Football, Not Fishing . . . So Build a Team You Can Trust

Attorney. Executor. Trustee. Personal and property guardians for your minor children. A healthcare attorney-in-fact for financial and healthcare directives including living wills. These are the people to whom you entrust your life, your loved ones, and your wishes. They are crucial to creating and maintaining family peace as well as keeping your estate plan intact. Yet the roles of these estate team members often overlap. This not only makes it hard to keep straight who does what, it also makes the decision-making for selecting each one exponentially harder. Some team members will help you create the documents (the planning phase), while others will be responsible for carrying out your wishes after you are gone (the administration phase). Some will be involved in both phases.

To help you sort through the maze, this chapter is divided into sections describing the roles and responsibilities of each significant player. To address the most common questions and concerns people have when putting together their team, every section ends with a checklist of questions to ask yourself or potential candidates before making your choice.

Who's the Quarterback?

If you did a search right now on the Internet and put in the words "quarterback in estate planning," a number of experts would lay claim to the role from attorneys to accountants to financial planners to banks to even insurance agents. This slew of service providers is constantly vying for your attention and money, all saying they will help you with your estate planning or entirely do it for you. They each claim if you go to them, "You won't have to worry about a thing!"

Despite what they might tell you, you can save yourself and your family a lot of heartache, pain, and expense by knowing this: Although these professionals provide critical advice and services, you and you alone are the quarterback during the planning phase! No one else. Most people make the assumption that the quarterback is the attorney or even a bank, but ultimately the choices are yours to make. While it's true that estate planning is definitely a team sport, you are the only one who holds all the information about what is most important to you. The teammates are there to help you realize your goals.

Here are the main players in the estate game:

- **Attorney:** Your attorney interprets and researches the law, drafts documents, reviews documents you've created, and advises you on meeting the legal requirements relevant to your situation. Instead of just telling you what you should or can't do, you need an attorney who will help you to identify and actualize your goals. In most cases an attorney is also involved in administering your estate.

- **Executor:** The most immediately visible member of the team after you are gone, the executor is primarily the administrator of the estate. He or she is responsible for making sure that the instructions in your will and all legal obligations are met.

- **Trustee:** If you have a trust, this player serves as the gatekeeper and administrator of the assets you have left in the trust. Trustees serve until they resign, they are removed, or the trust ends.

- **Guardian:** This team member assumes the role of parent for your minor children or loved ones who are unable to care for themselves.

- **Attorneys-in-fact:** These are agents whom you appoint to act for you under certain circumstances, generally when you are incapacitated, to make medical or financial decisions on your behalf. You define what powers these agents have and when they have them in documents called durable powers of attorney.

- **Others:** Beyond the previous five team members, many people also rely on accountants, stockbrokers, financial planners, bankers, private investment advisory firms, and insurance companies. But beware! These service providers may or may not be certified by a professional organization or their state. When deciding which other advisors to consult with, be sure to ask them similar questions to the ones used when selecting an attorney.

Not sure who you want to join the team? You are not alone! One of the most common reasons for leaving a will unfinished—or not starting one in the first place—is thinking you will be locked into decisions you make when picking players for the team. But remember that no matter whom you choose, little is set in stone. You can always develop contingencies, nominate backup successors, or completely change your mind about your selections.

Although you can change any of these players until the moment you are no longer able to make decisions, the goal is to find people who can stay involved from start to finish and with whom you can establish a long-term relationship based on mutual trust and confidence. When it comes to professional service providers, you'll find they are *not* equally competent, caring, fair with their rates, and efficient. So when you find ones you like, keep them! With regard to executors, trustees, and guardians—most often chosen from among family members and trusted friends—be sure to review your appointments on a regular basis and especially when big life events occur. Changes in their circumstances or your own may mean that someone else has become better suited for the job.

Once you are gone, the ball passes to the rest of the team. So make your choices carefully, but be sure to make them! Then go about your life knowing you've done your best to leave your family in peace. Now let's take a look at each of the significant players.

THE ATTORNEY

The primary duty of the attorney in estate planning is to provide legal advice and to draft legal documents such as wills and trusts. At the end of the day, your attorney's key concern is that you have complied with the law and minimized estate taxes, if any. Depending on the size of your estate and the attorney's expertise, he or she might also work with specialists (yours and/or ones they recommend) such as accountants and financial planners who can help address potential tax consequences of your estate plan.

Attorneys generally enter the will process at two key times: during the planning stage and after your death to help with the administration of your estate.

PLANNING

During the planning stage, attorneys are generally called upon for three functions. First, to draft a customized will and other estate documents that are appropriate for your circumstances and meet the legal requirements of your state. Second, to update your documents when these circumstances change. Marriage, divorce, the birth of children or grandchildren, death of a spouse, new dependents, and significant changes (up or down) in the value of your estate are common times for reevaluating who gets what and updating your documents. Third, people who draw up their own wills and other estate documents sometimes ask an attorney to review their work. Although some attorneys will automatically decline such requests, others—including through online services—will gladly consult with do-it-yourself will writers.

ADMINISTRATION

After someone's death, attorneys are likely to be involved with administering the estate. For example, if they have been working with the now deceased person for some time, they will likely enter the picture again to read the will and/or formally notify named beneficiaries. Often the executor will ask the attorney for help navigating through the maze of probate, taxes, and distribution of assets. Since wills go through a probate court, even if a trust has been established, an attorney usually handles court affairs to insure the estate is transferred in an orderly and legal fashion. Lastly, if disagreement breaks out over who gets what and the will is contested, each party involved—including the estate—will most likely have its own attorney.

You might be able to find a lawyer who can help you now and also advise your family after your death. But there is nothing to prevent your executor from choosing someone else to help your family through the estate administration phase. There are always two sides of a successful attorney–client connection: The attorney must be able to provide the needed expertise and counsel *and* you must be able to readily share your hopes and concerns with him or her. Your family might simply feel more comfortable with a different attorney than the one you had worked with, or the executor may want to work with someone closer to his or her home.

From my experience, I have found a tremendous amount of confusion when it comes to attorneys and estate planning. Here are the most common questions people have asked me on this subject.

Do I even need an attorney to create my will?

The short answer is this: it all depends on your situation. The general rule of thumb is the more complex your estate or situation, the more likely you will need to hire an attorney to customize your will. Many people—especially those with few assets and uncomplicated circumstances—have been able to create valid wills without hiring an attorney. Most lawyers who draft wills start with a form that contains the same types of clauses found in the readily available do-it-yourself will books, kits, or online services. That said, this area of the law can be confusing—creating a will yourself is not for the faint of heart. As one highly educated woman recently told me, "I tried one of the leading will kits using a CD on my computer. After reading everything, I attempted to insert my information. Immediately, I hit a stumbling block. It took me hours to backtrack and realize that my husband and I were expected to complete separate wills. I had missed the small print." As you might expect, lawyers aren't generally big fans of do-it-yourself methods. Some will refuse to work with you if you are writing your own will. Others, however, will charge a nominal fee for reviewing what you've created, sometimes with the hope of earning more significant fees later by administering the estate after you are gone—kind of like a loss leader.

Consulting an attorney becomes especially important when:

- You don't know the best ways to leave assets to loved ones, given your specific goals.
- Your estate has a total value of more than one million dollars.

- Your circumstances are complex. For example, you want your current wife to maintain possession of your home until her death, at which time you would like it to go to your children from a previous marriage and not to hers.
- You are leaving a small business to your children that you own with several others.
- You are leaving assets to an incapacitated dependent through a special needs trust.
- Early indicators suggest that your will is likely to be contested.
- You are thinking about disinheriting a child or spouse.

Should I look for an attorney who specializes in wills and estate plans?

Under ethics rules, an attorney must be competent to write a will before doing so. Theoretically, any attorney who has taken an estate law class has been trained to advise you about your will. But whether they are actually experienced is a whole other matter! And even when they specialize in this area, there is no guarantee of skill or compassion.

So the answer is this: rather than seeking out an attorney who specializes in wills and estate planning, simply inquire about his or her experience. Of course, those who specialize in estate planning are likely to have more experience in this area. Again, the general rule of thumb is the larger and more complex the estate, the more important it is to go to a specialist. For more basic wills, you can generally work with most any attorney with experience creating wills. One client was recently refinancing her mortgage when she got a call from a lawyer who was verifying the title on her property. He mostly worked for banks in real estate law. When the woman asked if he also helped with wills, he responded, "Yes, I do simple wills for estates under

$1 million in value. If it's worth more than that, you are better off working with a will and estate planning specialist. If that's the case, I know several attorneys I could recommend."

What if I have a special needs dependent? Do I need an attorney who specializes in that?

You can either hire an attorney who specializes in this area or ask the attorney with whom you are already working on your will to consult a specialist. In either case, if you have a son or daughter with a disability, you definitely want professional advice from someone who is familiar with the finer legal and tax points of these situations. Although the exact trigger number depends on a complex calculation, even an inheritance as small as $2,000 can disrupt the government SSI and Medicaid payments of a person with a disability. One way to address this problem is to speak with an attorney about setting up a Supplemental and/or Special Needs Trust (SNT). These trusts preserve eligibility for government benefits while leaving assets to meet the extra needs of your loved one. SNTs allow the trustee to have access to a variety of additional resources from medical treatment that Medicaid won't cover to recreational activities to a home to live in. For less wealthy parents, SNTs are often funded by the proceeds of an insurance policy.

What are the most important characteristics I should look for in an attorney?

Without a doubt, the most important characteristics are integrity, experience, and interpersonal communication skills.

Look for an attorney who is sensitive, creative, a good listener, honest, and won't sell you the same package he or she sells everyone else or services you don't need. Many people come to me saying, "I wanted to do this, but my attorney said that I couldn't." That is simply an unacceptable outcome. The attorney you work with should either help you do what you asked to do, or show you why it wasn't such a good idea and offer alternate ways to achieve the same goal. Experience is equally important. Seek an individual with training and expertise specific to your needs. But the last thing you want is a technical genius who is also cold, arrogant, or intimidating. Talking about your will often requires you to reveal highly personal and emotionally charged details about your family life. You want an attorney you can trust and communicate with—someone you feel comfortable asking questions to, no matter how basic or stupid they might sound.

How can I find an attorney with the right characteristics?

Other attorneys, even in unrelated practice areas, are often the best source for referrals. Ask an attorney you trust to tell you who handles his or her own estate planning needs. Professional communities are relatively small. If someone delivers excellent or substandard service, word gets around. By asking other attorneys, whomever you interview will likely feel accountable to the peer recommending them. Leveraging professional networks also works well for finding accountants, financial planners, and other estate planning services.

You can also talk to friends, relatives, and associates whose opinions you value. Ask them for a recommendation of an attorney with whom they have worked. Be warned, however, that their experience is generally limited to the one or two lawyers they have personally had contact with. Another way to find an attorney to help you with your will is to call a few local banks and ask someone in their trust department whom he or she uses and likes. You can also contact the state and county bar associations for referrals. They maintain lists available by phone and the Internet of local attorneys. The drawback of this approach is that these listings simply show answers to cursory forms but don't address experience. These same legal associations will usually be able to tell you if any complaints have been filed against the attorneys or their firm.

If I want a lawyer to work on my will, at what point in the process should I bring him or her in?

The attorney should be there from the get-go. But the clearer you can be to begin with about what you want to accomplish, the more easily he or she can help you. If your estate will be subject to taxes, it's especially important to consult an attorney early on in the process.

Can an attorney help me ward off family conflicts?

Although many attorneys stay within a comfort zone of legal forms and the tax code, others are excellent at guiding you through potentially explosive family dynamics. These are the advisors who ask you about your values and goals, offer creative approaches to sticky situations, encourage you to create legacy vehicles to more fully communicate with loved ones, take the time to fully explain their recommendations, and are able to maintain a calm and compassionate tone with your heirs.

What are the signs that I have hired the wrong attorney?

You just signed your will and you have little idea of
what it says, what it does, and how it does it. The attorney
doesn't answer your questions in language you can understand and doesn't listen to you or return calls. He or she
uses a cookie-cutter approach, little of which seems relevant to your situation. The attorney tries to write a role
for him- or herself into your will. You feel bullied into certain outcomes that the attorney thinks are best.

Will the attorney keep my original will?

Given how frequently lawyers change firms and clients
move around, it's becoming less and less common for attorneys to keep original will documents. Instead, many
people store theirs in a safety deposit box at the bank. If
you plan to do this, consider adding a loved one's name to
the safety deposit box account to avoid having the IRS
freeze it upon your death. Laws vary from state to state on
how and when the will can be taken out from the box in
such cases. Although in some states, such as Colorado, the
bank files the will with the local probate court, it's not always that simple to have your will filed. Consult an attorney or your bank about the practices in your state. If it's
not possible to file your will with the court and you don't
want a second person on your safety deposit box account,
you might be better off keeping the original in a fireproof
box or safe at home.

Some people create more than one original will (same
date, ink, and witnesses) so they can give one to their attorney and keep the second at home with their other estate
documents. Although having all estate documents in one
easily accessible place can prevent delays and hassles for

loved ones, having a second original requires extra caution when changing or revoking your will. Be sure to destroy all copies of the previous version. Whenever there's an older original floating around out there, you are setting the stage for litigation to prove which will is valid.

Whatever route you take for storing your will, remember the goal is to avoid confusion. If your original will cannot be found, the court presumes you revoked it unless there's sufficient testimony that it has simply been lost. If the court finds the will to be lost and not revoked, then a copy of it will most likely be followed.

What about fees?

Some attorneys offer a complimentary and brief up-front consultation while others will charge you for the first meeting. Charging or not charging for the initial consultation has to do with local custom or the firm's policy. Whether you are charged for this session or not, you should walk away with an understanding of what is needed to proceed and approximately how much it will cost. The fees will be based more on the complexity of your work together than on the actual value of the estate. Come prepared with all of your facts for the most accurate estimate of costs.

MAKING THE CALL

Here is a checklist of key questions to consider when you are in the process of selecting an attorney:

☐ Will the attorney give me a free consultation or will the attorney charge for the initial interview? If so, at what rate?

☐ If the attorney is part of a larger law firm and my estate is not complicated, can he or she recommend a senior associate with good experience who might be a better fit than the higher priced partner in the firm? (The standard term for this is "cost sensitive" as in I'm "cost sensitive" and do not think I can afford your rate. Can you recommend someone else, perhaps an experienced senior associate, to help me?)

☐ Will the attorney provide references of other attorneys and clients with whom he or she has worked in the past? (Try to get at least two or three names.)

☐ What percent of the attorney's practice is estate planning? What percent is estate litigation? How long has he or she been practicing in this area?

☐ Given what you tell the attorney your needs are, can he or she provide a ballpark figure of what similar services for other clients have run? What factors will affect the final cost of working together?

☐ How does the planning process work? Can the attorney walk you through what you do, what they do, and how to keep costs down?

☐ Can the attorney describe a typical client in his or her estate planning practice?

☐ Does the attorney seem more interested in your money than your goals?

☐ Does the attorney always seem in a hurry, act too busy, or sound condescending? How do you feel when you talk with him or her?

☐ Is the attorney able to explain him- or herself and the

law in ways that are easy to understand? Does the attorney answer your questions completely and thoughtfully?

☐ Are the fees the attorney charges proportionate to the size and complexity of your estate? Does the attorney offer you an inexpensive will as a loss leader with hopes of earning more later in administration fees?

☐ After describing your overall goals and what you'd like the end results to be, what does the attorney recommend for someone in your shoes? Will he or she give you a written letter describing how he or she would proceed?

THE EXECUTOR

An executor's job is to carry out the terms of your will. The work of an executor begins immediately upon your death and ends after the estate is distributed. This can take many months or even years depending on the estate's complexity, how well-organized you've left your affairs, and how clearly you communicated with others during the planning phase. Your choice as executor is the first thing people are going to hear when your will is read. If your estate is modest and there are no trusts or trustees involved, the executor assumes the position with the most power.

Naming an executor can be fraught with conflicts, not only in your own head but also in the minds of your loved ones. Although the role primarily consists of filling out forms and filing them, family members view it as a popularity contest as in, "I always knew he loved Billy or Sally best." One couple literally drew a name from a hat rather than face the prospect of deciding between their adult children. Others have decided to jointly appoint all of their children to serve as co-executors, while some choose a trusted friend. Ultimately, you must balance a desire to pick the best person for the job with your concerns about ruffling the feathers of loved ones who are not selected. Then you must be sure that whomever you choose, as well as any alternate, actually wants the job!

Some people get so hung up on making the key estate-planning decisions—such as who will be the executor—that they put off completing their wills. It's important to remember that nothing is written in stone. You can always include contingency clauses to address changing circumstances and, as long as you are still here, amend your will in what is called a codicil. The key is to make the best decision you can based on what you know *right now*.

The work of an executor is largely a thankless, tedious, detail-oriented job—but one that must be done responsibly and properly to speed the distribution of your estate. Heirs often misunderstand what being an executor is all about. Explaining the actual duties to your family beforehand, as well as the rationale behind your choice for filling this role, can go a long way toward keeping the peace.

To help guide you in your decision-making process, here are the questions I'm most commonly asked about executors.

What does an executor actually do?

An executor's job is to identify all of the estate's assets, pay off its debts, and file government forms including taxes. Additionally, the executor will distribute assets to the rightful heirs and beneficiaries according to the specifications in your will and other estate documents. When asking a family member or friend to serve as your executor, it's a good idea to share the following detailed list with them so they can fully grasp the responsibilities they would be agreeing to fulfill:

- Locate the will.
- Retrieve the death certificate.
- Hire a lawyer and/or accountant, if necessary.
- Apply to appear before the Probate Court.
- Notify beneficiaries named in the will.
- Send death notices to the post office, utilities, banks, and credit card companies.
- Complete a Change of Address form at the post office so that future mail addressed to the deceased is forwarded to the executor.
- Arrange for publication of notice to creditors and mail a notice to each known creditor.
- Pay valid claims against the estate.
- Collect debts owed to the estate.
- Check with the deceased's employer for unpaid salary, insurance, and other employee benefits.
- List the contents of any safety deposit boxes.
- Check insurance coverage of the deceased and file appropriate claims.
- Inventory all assets and have them appraised and/or stored as necessary.
- Determine a preliminary estimate of the estate's value.
- Collect data on all property owned by the estate that will not be part of the probate process; for example, property held in joint tenancy.
- File income and estate tax returns.
- Distribute assets and obtain receipts from beneficiaries.
- File all required papers to finalize the estate including an accounting of all transactions involving estate assets.

Does an executor always work with a lawyer or other professionals?

Usually, unless the estate is very simple and/or of little financial value, the executor likely will need to hire professionals to assist with taxes and other matters. You've picked someone you believe will have the common sense to know when they need help and how to seek additional resources including professional advice. Attorneys and accountants who work with the finer points of estate settlement and taxes can provide excellent counsel. But in the end, it will be the executor's call on how to interpret your instructions (or lack thereof) on everything from whether or not to sell a property to determining investment strategies for assets until they are distributed.

In your experience, whom do most people appoint as an executor?

It's different for every individual and every family. There is no one-size-fits-all solution. Some people choose a spouse, grown child, sibling, or other relative while others select friends or business associates. All or some of the adult children might be selected to serve as co-executors. Others choose a financial institution instead of a person, especially when the estate is complicated or family feuds already loom on the horizon. Financial institutions can also be named as a co-executor to act jointly with family members. Attorneys or accountants can be selected, but this is rarely done. When serving as executors, if they hire themselves to perform professional services, courts might find a conflict of interest. Most firms will turn down the request. Similarly, before appointing a business partner as executor, carefully consider potential conflicts of interest such as what value is assigned to the estate's share or decisions about selling the business.

What should I consider when choosing an executor?

First and foremost, you should choose someone who is honest and whom you can trust to carry out your wishes. As you can see from the previous laundry list of duties, there is a great deal of responsibility and time involved in acting as an executor. Consider the following:

Qualifications.   Your executor should be someone who is willing, able, responsible, organized, and detail-oriented. Additionally, he or she should be someone who has the time and lives nearby or is committed to being available when needed. Although having a head for numbers and good business sense are a definite plus, they are not requirements—unless the estate lacks the financial resources for the executor to hire legal and financial advice.

Personality.   An executor is very much of a figurehead and can set the tone for acceptance or resentment of your will, including heirs' attitudes toward each other and professional team members. As we've discussed throughout this book, the will can become a lightning rod for family disappointments. In your absence, frustrations can be unfairly directed at the executor, the person now in the power position. He or she might even be blamed as complicit or responsible for legal requirements or estate decisions to which he or she was never privy. If heirs are unhappy about something, they will point their fingers at the executor for any disparities (real or imagined).

Choosing an executor who is generally level-headed and noncombative by nature—someone who is perceived as honest, fair, and nonjudgmental—can greatly reduce the quantity and degree of conflict.

Time of Grief.   Given that they are immediately called into action, executors often say they have difficulty taking the time to grieve. By virtue of the role they have agreed to assume, and since going through Probate Court takes months or even years, they will be faced with constant reminders of your death for a long time to come. For this reason alone, some people prefer to pick someone outside of the family rather than burden their spouses or adult children with being the executor. As one client remarked, while no doubt there was a lot of paperwork and logistics, the real drain was the "ongoing reminder of my mom's absence."

Gender and Birth Order.   Some people automatically assign the executor role to the firstborn or male child. Think long and hard before walking down this road. I've seen many, many hard feelings created over choosing the executor simply on the basis of birth order or gender. One of my clients, a Wall Street father with three, very capable daughters—two of whom were stockbrokers and one a nonpracticing attorney—chose his salesman son to serve as executor. Upon learning this, the incensed daughters confronted both their parents head on. Mom wholeheartedly agreed with them. Dad was shocked, but retreated knowing he had underestimated his daughters and had been caught playing the sexist hand. He reconsidered and changed his will, naming the daughter with a law degree as executor.

Is appointing all my children as co-executors a good idea?

Again, it really depends on a number of variables. Do your children get along? If they don't, the administration of your estate will most likely suffer from the "too many cooks in the kitchen" syndrome. Will all of your children act responsibly and step up to the plate, or will one or more be saddled with most of the work causing animosity toward siblings? Equally important is the in-law card. For example, one woman wanted to name both of her children as executors but worried that her daughter's hard-to-please husband would meddle too much. She decided to name just her son as executor. There are also logistical concerns to consider. It can be quite inconvenient when children are dispersed across state lines and documents need to be signed. However, these days with e-mail and overnight delivery services, distance may not be as much of an obstacle as it once was. Even if having children share the executor position seems less than ideal, it's sometimes still the best choice *when* the decision generates more family harmony than discord. If you do go the co-executor route, be sure to predetermine how differences of opinion among them should be settled. Include in your will a "majority rules" or "tie breaker" clause for cases in which they can't come to an agreement.

Should I talk with the person I name as my executor beforehand?

Absolutely. You need to explain what he or she is getting into and ask whether he or she would be willing to accept the position. Remember, though, even if the person agrees, he or she is not obligated to act as your executor. A change in life circumstances might ultimately preclude that person or he or she might die before you, which is why people often avoid choosing their parents. This makes it all the more imperative to include in your will an alternate executor, often called a successor executor, someone who will act as executor if the first-named person cannot serve. Be sure to first ask the successor if he or she is willing to be appointed. If none of your selections for executor are able to act, the Probate Court will appoint one, usually a member of your family.

Should I pay my executor?

An executor has a legal right to charge the estate a fee but does not have to do so. This situation can cause a host of misunderstandings among loved ones, so it's important to sort out ahead of time whether a fee will be paid and, if so, how much it will be. An attorney or accountant can advise you as to what would be considered an appropriate amount in your state and for the value of your estate. Generally a maximum amount of 2 percent to 5 percent of the estate's gross value is allowed, depending on the state. Many states just use the words "reasonable compensation" with a host of case law to define what that means. Others set a schedule based on a percentage of the estate. In New York, for example, the allowed fee is 5 percent of the first $100,000 up to 2 percent on amounts more than $5 million. In all states fees can be increased when the executor is required to perform extraordinary services such as defending the estate against suits, selling assets, or handling audits.

Predetermining the fee not only makes it clear to the

executor what he or she will be paid, but also lets family members know that you want the executor to be compensated. In cases where estate taxes will be due, paying the executor can serve the additional function of reducing the tax bill of the estate. However, the fees received by an executor are taxable to them as personal income. In many cases family members will volunteer to administer an estate without taking a fee. But if you want the executor to be paid, it's best to specify an exact or maximum amount in your will. If this provision is not included in your will, the executor can still apply to the Probate Court for a reasonable fee. Whether determined by the court or by your will, if there is more than one executor, some states will have them share the fee—either splitting 50/50 or according to the work done by each. Other states allow each co-executor the entire allowable amount, potentially resulting in double or even triple fees.

In lieu of a cash payment, some families have found that leaving a possession of some value to executors is a more palatable way to compensate them. For example, one of my clients left one daughter his car in payment for her services as executor of the estate.

I'm confused. Some wills have executors and also trustees. What's the difference?

I'll get to trustees in the next section. Just know that when your estate plan includes both an executor and a trustee, ongoing financial power most often lies with the trustee. So, if in order to keep the peace, you feel the need to appoint a particular adult child or other family member to serve in some capacity, it's far wiser to compromise on your choice of an executor than on whom you name as a trustee. Remember, an executor only exists until the estate is distributed, while a trustee can stay in place for years or even decades.

MAKING THE CALL

Here is a checklist of key questions to ask yourself before choosing your executor or an alternate successor:

☐ Who is willing and able to do this in a time of shock and grief?

☐ Who has the stamina to work with the accountants and/or attorneys to file tax documents, along with the dedication to spend hours and hours doing this? Who will make sure it's done right?

☐ Who is likely to be responsible for fulfilling this role for the benefit of all?

☐ What signals would choosing this or that person send to other family members? Will the appointment of a particular executor have any damaging effects upon the family?

☐ Do I know what my children think? Have I mistakenly assumed that one of my children wants to be my sole executor to the exclusion of his or her siblings?

☐ If I plan to name my children as co-executors, do they work well together and will geographic distance cause an insurmountable inconvenience?

☐ Have I discussed this appointment with the person I have in mind and with the candidate for successor executor?

☐ Does the person I've selected fully understand the responsibility and time involved in being an executor? Do they agree to serve?

Finally, once you have made the decision, remember to ask yourself this: How can I communicate my choice to loved ones in a way that will minimize potential conflicts and ill feelings? For example, the following letter was written by one couple to their children as a way to explain who they picked as executor and why:

Dear Mark and Maria,

You have been our pride and joy. Although your mom and I know we haven't always been perfect people, it's been our intent to bring love into your lives. We know you have been asking questions about our plans now that we are retired. Instead of having a big, in-person family talk about it, we've written this letter with hopes that we can spend our precious vacation time together in July without this topic looming over us all.

We've been planning for years, and it looks like we'll have enough to live on for the rest of our lives. If we're lucky, there may be a little extra left in the house and from our savings after we both go. We don't want to go into details, but you should know we've decided to borrow against the house now and have it sold after we are gone. You two can split the proceeds and whatever else we might have left when we pass on. So don't quit your day jobs, kids, we're not talking about a lot of cash here. But we hope anything we have left might be helpful to you.

One more thing we'd like you to know is that
we've chosen Raymond Martinez to be our executor.
I know I'll be a wreck when your mom goes, and she
says the same about me. Rather than have you two
worry about dotting all the i's and crossing all the t's,
we would rather you spend time with the family to get
through the grief. We also know you two haven't
always agreed on things, so we thought this would be
a better way to go. Ray and his wife, Louisa, have
asked me to be their executor as well. Neither couple
wants family members to be put through the wringer
of being executor.

We've found out that being an executor is like
being the will's secretary and is a pretty thankless job
of filing documents, signing court papers, and so on.
But don't worry, Ray won't be making any decisions
about who gets what and when. Your mom and I have
figured all of that out ahead of time. Blame us and the
somewhat bizarre estate laws if you end up thinking
things should have been different. We've decided to
pay Ray $1,000 for his time, and he's agreed to pay
me the same. Looks like executors can take a nice
chunk of change out of the estate as a fee, but Ray
and I decided on this amount mostly as a way to show
our appreciation for each other.

If Ray passes before we do, Louisa didn't
want to be the executor. We don't feel comfortable
with anyone else, so we've named you two as
co-executors. You'll need to work together and
help each other. I know you two have butted
heads in the past, but fighting after we go will only
cost you grief and money—not to mention break our
hearts.

Since neither Ray nor I have done this before, we've agreed that as executor we would hire an attorney and an accountant that the estate will pay for.

Please call us with any questions you have.

We love you now and always,
Dad and Mom

THE TRUSTEE

While an executor's job comes and goes—ending when the estate has been administered—a trustee plays a more ongoing and ultimately powerful role of managing and disbursing the assets you've left to a spouse, child, grandchild, or other loved one in a trust. As the "keeper of the keys," the trustee bears a substantial responsibility for making decisions on your behalf after you are gone. The trustee is expected to follow the instructions and guidelines you lay out in your trust. However, much like the Supreme Court interpreting laws passed by Congress, the trustee must interpret your wishes and can wield a great deal of discretion in the process. It all depends on how clear you were in the first place and how well the trustee understands your intentions—along with how willing and able the trustee is to carry them out.

Trusts have become increasingly powerful and widely used tools in estate planning for minimizing taxes, keeping assets out of probate, planning for dependents, and providing financial security for families. The person or institution assigned to manage the trust is called the trustee. Given that trustees manage both the assets and determine when to pay out money to beneficiaries, this is one job you really need to have done right!

TRUSTS

Before we get more into what a trustee actually does and what you should consider when selecting one, let's first talk about what trusts are, why people decide to create them, and the basics of how they work.

What is a trust?

Contained in the will itself or written as a separate document, a trust sets up a relationship in which one person manages property for the benefit of another who actually owns the rights to it, the beneficiary. There are a multitude of trust types under all sorts of complicated names, which can make the entire concept seem quite confusing. (See sidebar: Common Trust Vehicles.) You can demystify all of this by simply thinking of the trust as a legal box in which you store the assets you want to give to people or organizations at some later time. You choose when and how. Then you select the people and/or financial institutions—called the trustee—who will hold the box, keep its contents safe, and manage the necessary legal/financial aspects. You also predetermine when and under what conditions the trustee can open the box to release its contents for the benefit of the beneficiaries.

Trusts can be created and funded during your lifetime (a living or inter vivos trust) or enacted only after your death under the terms of a will (a testamentary trust). At any given time, each trust is either irrevocable or revocable. A revocable trust can be changed after it has been established, whereas an irrevocable trust cannot. Most revocable trusts become irrevocable at some later time; for example, when the person who creates it dies.

Although living trusts can be revocable or irrevocable, "living trust" has become the increasingly popular term for a certain type of revocable trust people make to continue to control and use their assets while still alive and to keep the trust assets out of probate when they pass on. In this book, we'll follow suit by only using "living trust" in reference to this particular type of revocable trust. With a living trust, you are easily able to make changes as needed and can place property into one by simply changing the name of the asset's title. For example, if you want your home to be held in trust, you must prepare and sign a new deed transferring your home to "Bill Andrews, trustee of the Bill Andrews Revocable Living Trust dated September 4, 2005." Because the property included in a living trust must be distributed shortly after death, people often create additional and longer-lasting trusts to hold assets for beneficiaries named in the living trust itself and/or the will.

Whatever the type of trust, be certain to spell out your intentions as clearly as possible. Although you won't be able to think of and address every issue that could possibly come up, trustees will be forced to guess what you had in mind if you make vague statements in your trust like this: "Funds can be used for the purpose of health and welfare." The more specific you can be about your wishes when creating a trust the better.

Why do people create trusts in the first place?

There are a variety of motives for setting up a trust. Most people find they can easily benefit from one or more of the following reasons:

Keeping assets out of probate.   Probate is the default system for all assets not placed in trust or owned in certain other ways. Although your will must still go through probate, the assets you've placed in trust are excluded, making it a much quicker and less expensive process. A recent AARP study confirms that probate is slow and costly. Fees often consume up to 10 percent of the assets in even an uncomplicated, middle-class estate.

Another reason for keeping your assets in a trust and out of probate is to ensure that information about your assets and beneficiaries remains confidential. Everything contained in your will becomes public record during probate. As well, putting your assets in trust protects your loved ones from having their income interrupted while waiting for the probate court to act. Having a trust can also enable a going business to continue without disruption and without the need of a costly, court-appointed conservator to manage the assets.

Protecting assets. Trusts can be designed to protect assets in a variety of ways. For example, they can protect a beneficiary's inheritance from their creditors, a former spouse, or a current spouse in the event of an eventual divorce. Trusts also let you determine when young loved ones will be mature enough to manage assets for themselves. Sometimes a trust is created to temporarily or permanently manage the assets of an adult heir who has a track record of undesirable personal habits or spending practices.

Providing for dependents with special needs. Trusts can provide for loved ones with special needs, such as healthcare for a child with a disability or an elderly parent. Trusts designed to supplement benefits received by Social Security or welfare programs are generally called Supplemental and Special Needs Trusts. The rules for these trusts are quite complicated and require consultation with an attorney who specializes in this area.

Avoiding taxes.   Several kinds of trusts, including Marital Deduction Trusts, Irrevocable Life Insurance Trusts, Bypass Trusts, QTIPs, and Generation Skipping Trusts, help reduce or postpone estate taxes. If you face paying estate tax, it's advisable to discuss these options with an experienced attorney and/or an accountant.

Making charitable contributions.   Certain trusts enable you to donate assets to charities now and receive an income or other funds back during your lifetime. These include Charitable Remainder Trusts and Charitable Lead Trusts. Special tax issues must be considered when using these trust vehicles and can be best sorted out with an experienced attorney and/or accountant.

Restricting the flow of money.   Some trusts are set up to ensure that assets are used only for certain purposes and/or under certain conditions. Many people want to help their loved ones but worry that the money might be spent for undesirable purposes, so they create a trust limited to specific uses such as education or buying a house. You can also set certain conditions that a beneficiary must meet in order to receive the money, such as completing a graduate program by age 30. However, a court will only uphold these conditions if they do not violate public policy. Acceptable conditions include requiring the beneficiary to meet certain professional and educational goals or including a dollar match with earned income, whereas insisting on marriage or the practice of a specific religion is not permissible.

Preventing a challenge.   Trusts tend to hold up better than wills do against challenges. It's usually much harder to prove fraud, incompetence, or duress when a trust is involved, especially if the person who set up the trust was managing it during his or her lifetime.

What kinds of property can be placed in trust?

Again, it all depends on the trust and your specific situation. For a revocable living trust, almost any kind of property can be placed in it, such as bank accounts, real estate, vehicles, stocks, and bonds. Some items, such as insurance policies, retirement accounts, and so on, have their own special beneficiary forms. These transfer directly to whomever you name as beneficiaries on those forms and do not need to be put into a trust to avoid probate. If you wish these items to filter through the trust rather than passing directly to a person (for example, to a minor child), simply name the trust as the beneficiary.

If I have a trust, do I still need a will?

Yes, absolutely. The will is the only place you can name a guardian. Also, certain assets—such as furniture and other personal possessions—do not lend themselves to being placed into a living trust. It's simply not practical or possible to put everything in a trust, no matter how carefully you set one up. A will also serves as a safety device in the event your trust were to be found invalid.

COMMON TRUST VEHICLES

Here are brief descriptions of some of the most commonly used types of trusts. They might sound complicated because they *are* complicated! Trusts can have significant ramifications on taxes and on your family. Be sure to consult an attorney to help you set them up correctly.

Asset Protection Trust: A trust designed to protect the assets of the person who sets it up from his or her creditors while still allowing the person to own and use the assets he or she places in it. These trusts are often called by the name of the state in which they are set up; for example, the Delaware Trust or the Alaska Trust. Asset protection trusts are typically used only by those with estates having a large value and are easily confused with more widely used **Protective Trusts.** These are established to protect the assets you give a loved one from his or her own behavior, creditors, and marriage or divorce. The protective strength of the trust depends on which kind you use.

Bypass Trust or Credit Shelter Trust: These trusts are used by married couples whose assets are likely to exceed the threshold for owing taxes under current federal law. When one spouse dies, bypass trusts allow the surviving partner to inherit the assets tax free, regardless of their total value. Then, when the second spouse dies, the estate can use the combined tax exemption from both individuals when determining what estate taxes, if any, would be due at that time. The surviving spouse has flexibility with what happens to trust assets.

Bypass trusts are often used with **Marital Deduction Trusts** and **QTIP Trusts** (Qualified Terminable Interest Property) when the person who sets up the trust wants to give his or her spouse all the income from the trust assets but still control who the final beneficiaries are. These trusts are designed so that the property in them passes to the spouse without taxation (under the marital deduction), the surviving spouse receives income from the property for life, and the person setting up the trust decides who the final beneficiaries are.

Charitable Trust: Different kinds of trusts can provide benefits to the person who created them and accomplish a gift to charity at the same time. They vary based on when the charity takes ownership of the property and what, if anything, the person setting up the trust receives back while still alive. Each type has its own tax impact. Two common ones are the **Charitable Lead Trust,** in which the charity receives income from the property for a fixed number of years after which the property goes to whatever beneficiaries were named, and the **Charitable Remainder Trust.** With this one, the person setting up the trust receives income during his or her lifetime and the charity receives the property upon death.

Dynasty Trust: An irrevocable trust designed to last for several generations.

Generation Skipping Trust: A trust designed to give assets directly to grandchildren with the option of giving children the right to income from the trust assets for their lifetimes. It eliminates the extra layer of estate tax that would occur if the property were left to children who would only later leave it to grandchildren. It also ensures that the grandchildren actually receive the trust assets at some point.

Grantor Trust: Because the person who sets it up keeps some kind of control or benefit, this trust is taxed as if the person who established it still owns the property him- or herself.

GRITs, GRATs, GRUTs: Specific types of irrevocable grantor trusts that give the person who set them up certain income or property use rights for a fixed time, but then transfer the trust assets to other beneficiaries at a certain point. These are taxed at a discounted value as gifts to the final beneficiaries when the trust is set up. This prevents estate or gift tax liability in the future on any increase in value from the trust creation onward.

Irrevocable Life Insurance Trust: A trust established to minimize estate taxes on insurance benefits.

Living Trust: A trust you can set up in addition to your will that lets you put things in and take things out now while you are still alive. A living trust can be changed or revoked until death, at which time the property goes to the beneficiaries you choose. Some states still use the Latin phrase "inter vivos trust." Property you put in a living trust does not go through probate but passes directly to the beneficiaries.

Supplemental and Special Needs Trusts: These allow you to provide assistance above and beyond the public benefits a loved one receives or may later receive due to age, disability, or any other qualifying reason without affecting their eligibility for those benefits. These are best handled by specialists in this complex area of law.

Testamentary Trust: Any trust you set up in your will as opposed to a separate, independent trust document.

TRUSTEES

Now that you are familiar with the common types of trusts and reasons for creating them, here are the questions I am most often asked about trustees.

What are the roles and responsibilities of a trustee?

These will vary depending on the nature of the trust. The following list includes the types of duties and obligations a trustee generally has:

- Manage assets and make investment decisions.
- Maintain records and report to beneficiaries.

- Prepare and file taxes.
- Follow the directives you wrote in the trust.
- Act as gatekeeper for who gets money and when.
- Interpret your intentions.
- Abstain from using funds from the trust for personal gain, monetary or otherwise. For example, a trustee can't invest in his son's new company with the money in your trust—even if that son happened to be Bill Gates!
- Make value choices that protect family harmony, not just the assets.

Who can serve as trustee?

Any person can be designated as a trustee. Many select a spouse, adult child, or relative while others prefer a friend, business associate, or outside professional advisor. Frequently, two or more individuals—often the adult children—are selected as co-trustees. An institution, generally a bank or private trust company, can be appointed instead of individuals or in addition to them as co-trustee. Institutions are most usually involved with larger and/or more complicated trusts. They are also brought in to maintain impartiality or to minimize emotional concerns. Since a trustee has quite a bit of discretion, some people prefer a blended solution. For example, when minor children are the beneficiaries of a trust, it might be a good idea to use a family member as co-trustee along with an institution to manage the assets. Trustees can also be given the authority to hire a third party to handle certain administrative functions like investing, accounting, and legal advice.

Similar to an executor, it's important to choose someone as an alternate, known as a successor trustee, in case your first choice can't serve. If the trust is expected to have a long-term existence, be sure to specify a process for choosing successor trustees down the road. Consider making the plan flexible enough to include family members as trustees in the future who may be too young to serve now.

When choosing a trustee or co-trustee, watch out for real or perceived conflicts of interest. For example, one client recently named his older daughter from a first marriage as the trustee of his estate instead of his second wife. His wife felt very uncomfortable at the thought of having to go to her stepchild for money. Further, there is an inherent conflict of interest: any assets unused by the wife during her lifetime will be inherited by her stepdaughter. This certainly creates an incentive for the daughter to deny the stepmother's requests for money! The whole situation has already caused a deep divide in the family. The stepmother has asked her husband to name a third party as trustee instead of his daughter to avoid major conflicts down the road.

Why are people sometimes wary of using financial institutions or trust companies as trustee?

Financial institutions can be excellent trustees, especially for large or complicated trusts and those with many beneficiaries who might not see eye to eye. However, here are a few things to consider. Many financial institutions will decline to serve as trustee if the assets involved are under $250,000 or even $500,000. Quite a few will also refuse an offer to serve as co-trustee with a family member. If you find yourself in either of these situations, consider the smaller, neighborhood institutions or private trust companies. The service and attention you are likely to get from an institution is unfortunately tied to the size of the estate.

The loaner apartments and cars, for example, that trust companies shower on very wealthy beneficiaries don't trickle down to heirs with more modest trusts. Smaller trusts are at greater risk for higher turnover, junior management, lower priority, and less attention from an institutional trustee. Buyer beware. Even the nice little trust department at your local bank is typically less geared to serve customers with only modest-sized estates.

The fees involved with using an institution as trustee are another concern and can significantly reduce the value of your trust. Also, banks tend to be more conservative with investments, meaning that your assets might not increase as quickly. They are less likely to consider higher-risk, higher-growth stocks or other investments, preferring bonds and blue-chip stocks instead.

The bottom line is that, although they care about their clients, serving as trustee is first and foremost a money interest. While legally an institution must uphold high standards of care, it's difficult to sue one if your co-trustees or beneficiaries are disappointed in the performance. It does not have to perform well. The bank or company need only find a defense for how it has acted reasonably under the circumstances. So when choosing an institution as trustee, consider including a provision in your trust for how it can be replaced by your heirs or a co-trustee if the need arises.

Can I name myself as trustee?

Generally you wouldn't be your own trustee except with a living trust. In most living trusts, people start off by naming themselves as trustee and maintaining control over the assets until death or until otherwise unable to serve. You must name a trustee to take over when you no longer can serve, someone to distribute assets in the manner established in your trust agreement.

You can't serve as trustee for any trust that is part of your will, however, because the trust won't even go into effect until after you are gone! Also, if you were to put your assets in a trust and then retain certain management or ownership benefits, you would likely lose any tax benefits the trust might otherwise provide.

What characteristics should I consider when choosing a person as a trustee?

Integrity. First and foremost, name a person you totally trust—someone who exhibits good faith, is honest, and has impeccable integrity. You want someone who understands you and shares your overall values because that person will inevitably have to interpret your instructions and make very important choices.

Hard skills. Legal, accounting, and business management skills are useful—all the more so if the trust is sizeable and complex. Although the trustee does not need to be an expert in these areas, it's wise to choose someone who is financially responsible and has shown the ability to make sound decisions on financial matters, particularly when investments are involved. At the very least, this person should have the ability to work with professional advisors.

Soft skills. Equally important are the soft skills, such as being able to encourage teamwork, solve problems, maintain good relationships with beneficiaries, and facilitate decision making. It's not unusual for an individual to name a friend with the requisite hard skills only to find that a spouse or children dislike or don't trust him or her. Try to avoid this by first discussing your potential choice with family members. If they are uncomfortable with the person or people you are considering, try to find someone else who has the hard skills but can also maintain a good rapport with heirs. If this is not possible, consider naming co-trustees for a balance between the business and relationship aspects. In this case, you might name an institution to provide the hard skills and an individual as co-trustee to provide the soft ones.

Availability.   Excellent personal qualities, hard skills, and soft skills are not enough! The person must also be willing and able to dedicate the necessary time and attention required of a trustee.

How long does a trustee serve?

The length of service is dictated by the terms and conditions you establish in the trust. The trustee role can last for a lifetime. If you have an institutional trustee, like a bank or family office, these agents can theoretically go on almost indefinitely.

Can the trustee be the same person as the guardian for my minor children? Should they be?

They can be the same person, but be aware that the role of a trustee is quite different from the parenting role of a guardian. As you will see in the upcoming section on guardians, the questions posed for choosing a guardian are very different from those for selecting a trustee. You might pick a dedicated family member as trustee who is a genius in the financial realm but is ill-suited to actually raise your kids. Although some advisors recommend not using the same person as both trustee and guardian for minor children, it really depends on your own situation. The pros and cons of naming the same person are explored in greater detail in the guardian section.

Is the trustee I name required to serve?

When push comes to shove, some people change their minds about wanting to take on the responsibilities and personal liability of serving as trustee. Once the trust goes into effect, the trustee you have named can say no at that time by filing a "declination to act" with the court. But if someone begins to serve as trustee and then decides to step down, he or she can only do so with a court's approval unless your trust document gives them the right to resign and name a successor.

What about liability?

Under state law, a trustee is a "fiduciary," meaning he or she must act with the highest standards of honesty and good faith. So if a disgruntled family member sues a trustee and the court finds the trustee at fault, the trustee must personally pay damages to the beneficiaries. Even though charges of inappropriate behavior against trustees are hard to prove, who wants the hassle? Worse yet, a trustee can also be personally liable for the misdeeds or mistakes of the previous trustee unless he or she corrects the predecessor's slipups by suing the predecessor or some other means. With co-trustees, each trustee is liable for the actions of the others. This exposure to liability can discourage institutions from taking on trust accounts in the first place, from acting as co-trustee with individuals, and from making anything but the most cautious investments or payouts to beneficiaries.

Are trustees entitled to fees?

Like executors, trustees have the right to charge "reasonable" fees for the work they do. Unlike executors, trustee fees are not typically spelled out by the state as a specific percentage of the trust. Private individuals often serve for free but have wide discretion in the amount they are allowed to charge if they choose. Unless a beneficiary brings suit to challenge their fees, they typically stand as long as they aren't significantly different from those charged by financial institutions. People often prefer to set a trustee fee in the trust document itself. That way if the named trustee agrees to serve, the amount has been predetermined for all to see. For example, "I agree that if Uncle Jim serves as trustee, he will receive $200 per year during his tenure."

When financial institutions serve as trustee, they generally charge an annual fee equal to a percentage of the trust's value, usually no more than 5 percent. It's not uncommon to be charged a higher percent for smaller trusts. Shop around. Fees can be substantially different from institution to institution and often are negotiable. Just be sure to get the fee agreement in writing.

Because each co-trustee can be liable for the actions of the others, in some states each co-trustee can take a full and separate fee rather than share what might be considered one "reasonable" fee. If co-trustees are involved, it's particularly important for you to predetermine their fees by stating them in the trust agreement. Trustee fees are always paid from assets in the trust, unlike executor fees that are paid with funds from the gross estate.

How can you remove a trustee?

Here an ounce of prevention is worth a pound of cure. Once the trustee agrees to serve, only a court order can remove him or her unless you include protections in the trust itself.

For a court to remove a trustee, a beneficiary must bring suit and claim "cause." A trustee has a fiduciary duty to act with honesty and in the very highest good faith. Less than optimal management, however, is not cause for removal. Although each state has its own cases as guidelines, some examples of cause are incapacity, conviction of a crime, serious risk of loss or loss itself to the beneficiaries, failing to file tax returns, and taking money from the trust.

When establishing the trust you can build in certain protections against a bad trustee. These include giving a beneficiary the right to remove and replace trustees in certain cases; for example, when a person acting as trustee no longer lives in the same state as the beneficiary or is experiencing extreme personal problems such as addiction or divorce. However, be aware that giving beneficiaries certain powers can have tax implications. Be sure to consult with an attorney. When an institution is the trustee, you can also specify removal under certain circumstances, such as a takeover/sale/merger of the company, too much turnover in trust management, or excessive fee increases.

How can I protect my beneficiaries in the trust document?

Protective measures can be directly written into the trust document and include:

- Giving power of appointment to someone so that he or she can remove assets from the trust and put them in a different trust or amend the trust. This power can be given to anyone and is intended as a watchdog device.
- Requiring the trustee to give each beneficiary an annual accounting of the trust accounts and/or post a bond.
- Expressing that the trustee should hire professional financial managers. This forces the trustee to do it and keeps heirs from getting upset at the expense.
- Designating a spouse or loved one as co-trustee with a financial institution and giving that person the right to approve a successor corporate co-trustee.
- Naming a "protector," someone other than trust beneficiary or trustee, who can check up on the trustee as the ears and eyes of the beneficiary. An example of this kind of action would be giving the protector the right to be able to remove and replace a financial institution as trustee.
- Making provisions that allow family members or other co-trustees to remove and substitute an institution serving as co-trustee with another if the beneficiaries are unhappy with the services being provided. Some people eliminate the potential of this problem by simply having the institution perform the functions as a service provider without being named as a co-trustee.

MAKING THE CALL

Here is a checklist of issues to consider during the process of selecting an individual as your trustee:

☐ Can I trust this person to be attentive, thorough, caring, scrupulously honest, timely, and focused on the well being of the beneficiaries?

☐ Does the person understand the responsibilities of being a trustee and is he or she willing to carry them out?

☐ Does the person have the health, capacity, and competency to serve? If so, for how long? Can I imagine under what circumstances the person might need to step down from being trustee? Who would be able to take over for him or her?

☐ Will the person bring enough financial sense to invest and manage trust assets—or at least enough common sense to hire experts who can advise him or her as needed (to be paid for by the trust, on behalf of the trust)?

☐ Do I and the person share a similar investment philosophy? If not, is the person willing to follow one that I spell out in the trust document (for example, 50 percent growth equities and 50 percent bonds)?

☐ Does the person have similar enough values to mine, such that he or she will be likely to interpret my guidelines in ways that are in keeping with my intentions?

☐ What kind of relationship does this person have with the beneficiaries? Is there a foundation of mutual respect? Is it likely that a positive business relationship can be developed if one is not already in place?

☐ Does this person understand the lifestyle, needs, and personalities of the beneficiaries?

☐ How will picking this person affect existing relationship dynamics? What family political ramifications might he or she face as trustee? For example, is this person strong enough to withstand potential aggression by trust beneficiaries who want the cash to flow more quickly than I've instructed in the trust document?

☐ Does this person have any conflicts of interest? (For example, one son is the trustee for all grandchildren. He might be tempted to draw more money for his own kids than his sister's unless the trust document prevents this with specific instructions.)

If you are planning to choose a financial institution—instead of, or in addition to, an individual—here are questions to ask:

☐ What fees does the institution charge and how often can the fees change? What services will my trust receive for those fees?

☐ Is there a good fit between the particular firm and the size/service needs of my trust? What types of trusts does the firm typically deal with?

☐ Who is the face with whom the beneficiaries will interact? How much attention will this person give my trust? Who will handle the trust when the original person is no longer available? How long has this person been working there and how much turnover in personnel does the company have? What happens to my trust if the firm merges or is sold?

☐ How well does this firm's investment philosophy (mix of assets and type of investments) match my own?

☐ What decision-making procedure is in place for making investments?

☐ What investment performance has the firm earned on its trust accounts in the past?

☐ How will the institution determine how much to pay out and when to pay it based on my instructions in the trust document? How will the firm interpret my guidelines? Will the firm cave in to or ignore requests from the beneficiary for more money?

☐ Will the firm accept serving as a co-trustee with a family member or working with a "protector," a third party who is asked to act as the eyes and ears of the beneficiary?

Here are questions to ask when considering co-trustees:

☐ Assuming each candidate can stand on his or her own after the above questions, can they work together? Are they willing to consent to work together given that each will be personally liable for the actions of the other(s)?

☐ How do I want disagreements to be resolved? Given the candidates, should I give one of them the power to remove and to appoint a successor co-trustee in case one can't serve anymore or the trustees become deadlocked? Should I put a tie-breaker mechanism into the trust itself to avoid the expense and bother of ending up in court?

☐ Is the benefit of having these candidates serve together greater than the risk of disagreement, acrimony, or deadlock?

☐ What does each co-trustee contribute? Can I achieve the same benefits by having one trustee and instructing that he or she hire professionals to help with specific areas?

THE GUARDIAN

One of the most universal concerns for people with young children is this: Who will raise their kids if the unthinkable happens and both parents die? Choosing someone to fill your shoes is rarely an easy task, especially given that spouses often have very different ideas about who would be the best choice. Choosing a guardian, however, is definitely something you shouldn't dally over or endlessly delay. Failing to name one invariably creates a free-for-all. Even worse, the judge could end up playing Mommy and Daddy until things get squared away, causing more emotional upheaval for the children during a time of immense shock and loss. The will is the only legal document in which you can nominate a guardian for your minor children (those under the age of 18).

There are actually two types of guardianship: a personal guardian and a property guardian. The personal guardian is an individual who takes physical custody of your children and is legally responsible for their care including food, clothing, and shelter along with making education and healthcare decisions. The personal guardian essentially picks up where you left off in raising your children.

Every minor must have a personal guardian. In addition, minor children also need someone to be responsible for any money or other resources you leave them. This person is called a property guardian or guardian of the estate. It's often more convenient to have the same person serve both functions—care of the children and overseeing their assets—but this isn't always the wisest choice. For example, your friend is a fabulous parent who would do an excellent job of raising the children, but your brother is savvy with investments and would be better able to handle their finances.

Whether it's the same person who raises them or not, once you've decided who will manage your minor children's inheritance you have two options. Either you set up a trust, which is what most people do, or use an antiquated vehicle called guardian of the estate. Unless waived in the will, a guardian of the estate must post a bond—the amount depends on the size of the inheritance—to reimburse the children in the event their inheritance is mismanaged. The guardian of the estate must also petition the court to spend the estate's money for certain expenditures on behalf of the children. You can save plenty of headaches by authorizing specific expenditures right in the will—from private school and summer camp to counseling, if need be. The guardian of the estate must also file regular accounting reports to the court. Generally, unless a suit is filed, these reports are not reviewed by anyone and simply create unnecessary paperwork. In some states, reporting requirements are so strict that the guardian must file each semester when tuition is due for a child who is attending a private elementary school.

Setting up a trust, as discussed previously in this chapter, not only sidesteps the cumbersome petitioning and reporting requirements a guardian of the estate must comply with, but also allows for continued restrictions on when and how an inheritance is disbursed once your child is no longer a minor. Another drawback to the guardian of the estate option is that when the child turns 18, he or she will automatically receive any remaining assets outright. It scares most parents to think what an 18-year-old might do if handed a check for, say, $100,000!

When it comes to naming the personal guardian, whether that person is also managing the finances or not, it's always better to name just one person instead of a couple to minimize the potential for a painful court proceeding should they end up in "Splitsville." For example, instead of naming your brother, Jeff, and his wife, Jill, just nominate Uncle Jeff. If you feel strongly that your children should be raised in a two-parent household, you can address this in your will with a statement such as, "I appoint my sister Louise to be guardian if she is married at the time of my death; otherwise, my cousin Janet . . ."

Parents should also make certain that their individual wills specify the same people as guardians and contingent guardians. Naming different people—or failing to provide a convincing rationale for your choice—leaves the door wide open for a challenge after you are gone. Even without a challenge, be aware that your request will not automatically be granted. Although usually honored, a court must still determine whether the guardian named by the parents serves the best interest of the children. For this reason, it is imperative that you supplement your will with specifics about how you know the named guardian, why you have selected him or her, and why he or she would be the best person to raise your children. Thoughtful documentation of your reasoning will help convince the judge to follow your wishes. This becomes especially important in situations where you expect someone to object to your decision. For example, Josie and Greg named their best friend as guardian, greatly offending Greg's sister and raising concerns that she would fight to gain custody of their two children. So Josie and Greg each included a detailed statement in their will explaining why they believe their friend is the better choice.

Here are some common questions posed by parents who are trying to select the best possible guardian in order to protect the fate of their children.

What are some of the most important factors to consider when choosing a personal guardian?

It's up to you to decide which characteristics and aspects are most important when choosing a guardian. This is a highly personal decision that only you and, if you are married, your spouse can make. Most parents begin the process by simply asking themselves, "Who would make the most loving parent?" After putting together a short list (each parent creates one), they factor in the issues below.

Values. Do his or her overall values, attitudes and lifestyle reflect your own and what you want for your children?

Religion. Does he or she have similar religious beliefs as your own?

Age. Does he or she have enough years still ahead to see your children through to adulthood?

Health.   Is the person healthy enough—both mentally and physically—to have the energy and stamina necessary for raising your children?

Experience.   How experienced is the person with children? If he or she is a parent, do his or her own offspring seem happy and well adjusted?

Personality and Patience.   Can the person handle the emotional responsibility and daily grind of raising your kids?

Marital Status and Stability.   Are there two partners in the home? Does the couple's relationship seem strong?

Family Ties.   Will the person encourage your children to spend time with your family members, even ones the guardian might not get along with or be related to themselves? Will the person keep in contact with your family if he or she lives halfway across the country?

Current Relationship with Children.   Is the person already close to your children, or is he or she a relative stranger? If the person and your children are not close yet, will it be possible for them to develop a relationship soon?

Playing Favorites.   If you have more than one child, does the person play favorites, or does he or she treat all the kids equally?

Location.   Where does the person live? Would he or she consider moving to your area if he or she lives far away to spare your children further upset by having to relocate?

What Your Kids Think.   Would your children be pleased with this choice? If you are unsure—and if they are mature enough—ask them! Some states do in fact allow children over 14 years of age to have a voice in the selection of their guardian and to exercise veto power.

Fitting Into the New Household.   Will there be other children already in the household? What ages are they? Would your children fit in or get lost in the shuffle? Does the potential guardian have the skills to keep peace and foster loving relationships between his or her children and yours?

Economic Realities.   Can the person take care of all of your children? Can he or she afford this role? By accepting your children, will the person require a bigger house or car? Will your estate be able to provide these for the guardian?

Economic Disparities.   Whether the estate is large or small, will there be an economic disparity—or a situation of have and have-nots—between the guardian's children and yours that might cause discomfort? Will the guardian's children go to private schools while your children will not, or vice versa? If your estate is able to provide your children with funding for travel or summer camps, will the potential guardian be able to provide the same for his or her own children or can you do so in the estate?

When should we talk to the potential guardian and what should we say?

After weighing in the various factors mentioned above, narrow the field and arrive at two or three suitable candidates. Then it's time to approach the first person on your list for a frank conversation. Don't limit the discussion to just the emotional aspects. Be sure to reveal pertinent financial details about the resources that will be available to help him or her bring up your children. Don't be surprised or harbor a grudge if your first pick declines. You would be putting your children in a difficult and painful, if not disastrous, situation if someone takes on the task of raising them without being fully committed. Beware as well that some family members might say yes out of guilt or a fear of offending you, even though they really want to say no. Make it comfortable for them to say no, so that when they say yes you know they really mean it. Be certain the person not only really, really understands the magnitude of the role, but freely embraces it.

Once you have a commitment from the guardian, describe in depth how you would want the children raised. These wishes can also be included in a separate letter or video to the nominee as well as any fallback candidates.

Can I name a different guardian for each of my children?

Most people choose the same guardian for all of their children because they want them to stay together. But if you believe that it will better meet your children's needs, you can name separate guardians for each of them. People with blended families that include children from different marriages with separate sets of relatives and those with a special needs child are more likely to consider this option.

Is it best that the guardian be a blood relative?

While many people do choose family members, a guardian can be anyone. More often than you might think, people deem close friends the better choice, particularly if they have a parenting style more aligned with their own and/or a more ongoing involvement in the children's lives. Don't feel guilty if you genuinely believe that someone outside of the family would do the best job.

As a same-sex couple raising children together, what should we be aware of when selecting a guardian?

Ideally both partners have legal rights as parents. Sometimes this can be accomplished through second-parent adoption, also called same-sex adoption or co-parent adoption. Intended to address situations in which unmarried partners share parenting duties yet only one of them is the child's legal parent, this serves to protect parental rights for the surviving partner. Adoption also ensures the legal right of the children to inherit from both parents and their respective families, providing for future financial stability. However, second-parent adoption is not always easy to obtain and two states, Florida and New Hampshire, have specific statutes prohibiting gay and lesbian adoptions. In cases where joint parental rights have not been established, it is critically important for the parent with legal status to accompany a nomination of the surviving parent as guardian with extensive supporting documentation of why this choice is in the best interest of the children. It is not uncommon for relatives to contest guardianship under these circumstances, so the stronger the evidence the better.

What happens if I don't want my child's other parent to be his guardian when I die?

If you are separated or divorced and your child's other parent survives you, then that parent usually assumes guardianship unless you make a strong case otherwise in a letter attached to your will. Courts typically grant custody to the other legal parent unless it can be proven that the surviving parent has abandoned the child by not providing for or visiting the child for an extended period or is unfit due to serious problems such as chronic drug or alcohol use, significant mental illness, or a history of child abuse.

Is it unwise to nominate my parents?

Most lawyers recommend against appointing one of the spouse's parents—or in other words, the grandparents—as guardians for the simple reason that in all likelihood they will predecease you.

Some people take heed of this advice while others ignore it. For example, the Greens of Fort Lauderdale decided against naming the children's grandparents noting, "Our criteria included someone who could raise our child in a way that is similar to our current family life and that's not realistic for grandparents in their 70s." On the other hand, Debbie and Bill of Portland came to a different conclusion. They appointed her parents as guardians because, "It made the most sense. They are living close by, healthy and active in their late 50s. Besides, they are already very involved in our daughter's life."

Naturally, you want to avoid selecting someone who is elderly, in poor health, or unable to actively care for your children. If you do nominate a set of grandparents, make sure that they will actually embrace this responsibility. While they may adore their grandchildren, will they still love them when they have to lay down the law about curfews or loud music, or worry about the financial drain on their retirement? It's important to ask for and seek out the truth.

Keep in mind that you always have the option of specifying in your will that guardians be designated on a contingency basis or for a set period of time. For example, you could indicate that if Grandma Lewis is physically unable to serve, then you elect Aunt Suzie. If you fear that your parents may grow too frail to handle being permanent caretakers, you can also specify that they serve as guardians until your child reaches a certain age after which guardianship passes to another person. Carefully consider, however, the impact of such a switch on your child.

Once someone has agreed to be a guardian, is that person legally bound to serve?

A guardian is not legally obligated to serve, even if he or she previously agreed to do so. People back out far more often than you might think. It's important to specify in your will second or even third fallback guardians should the first choice become unable or unwilling to serve.

Is a guardian paid for his or her services?

If you want to pay a guardian, consider setting up a trust making the guardian the beneficiary. This way you can clearly establish when and how much to pay for all to see. When the guardian is also the trustee of your children's trust, you can compensate him or her as part of the trustee fee.

What if my spouse and I can't agree on who to name as guardian?

Start by individually writing down your top three to five candidates. Then share your lists and have a frank discussion about why you each prefer your choices and what concerns you have about your spouse's selections. After exchanging this information, create a common set of characteristics you both agree are important. Now review the names on your own lists and see if you would like to make any changes, keeping these characteristics in mind. Compare revised lists to see if you now have some overlapping candidates. If so, work to create a joint list in order of priority. If you've made it this far, you are probably getting unstuck and are ready to start talking to potential guardians.

If you find you are still in a deadlock, however, it's probably time to bring in a third party to help you work through your differences. Find someone who is not in the running for guardian and has no stake in the outcome. Although a trusted friend or family member sometimes works, a minister or therapist is often the better choice. No matter how far apart you might seem, it's important to keep trying until you reach agreement. Focus on what's best for the children, not necessarily what's best for you as individuals or the family political situation. Remember that you can choose a successor guardian, add contingency clauses to address certain concerns that either of you might have, or change your mind about the nomination at any time. Some couples find they can reach agreement by appointing one person's top choice as personal guardian and the other's favorite pick as property guardian. However hard it might be to reach consensus, no choice is always the worst choice of all!

What are the advantages of selecting a different person for property guardian?

While most people do name the same person to be their child's personal guardian and to oversee the finances (as property guardian or trustee), others decide to separate the responsibilities. In some cases it's simply difficult to find one person who has both the parenting and the money skills. Another reason for dividing up the two roles is that a personal guardian might not want the additional responsibility of managing the finances, preferring instead to get a check every month for child-rearing expenses. Sometimes couples might simply want to spread out the responsibilities to another family member, hoping to thwart possible hard feelings as a result of not naming that person personal guardian. An argument can also be made that serving in both roles can create a potential conflict of interest, given that acting as property guardian could enable the guardian to make spending decisions for personal benefit using the children's assets, which could go unnoticed by the court.

Although some say that keeping the roles of personal and property separate creates a checks-and-balances approach and allows the two parties to use each other as a sounding board for financial and child-care decisions, the outcome entirely depends on how well the two people can work together. In many cases, having two people involved unnecessarily complicates matters.

MAKING THE CALL

When choosing a personal guardian, use this checklist to make sure you cover all the bases:

☐ Think carefully about whom I would like to raise my children should my spouse and I both die.

☐ Consider people whom I trust, have spent time with, and am certain have or can establish a good relationship with my children.

☐ It's usually best to choose someone who shares my attitudes, values, beliefs, and outlook.

☐ How will my children fit into the person's existing household?

☐ Consider the financial demands that my children will create on the guardian's life and make provisions accordingly.

☐ Choose someone a court would most likely approve: a good member of the community with no criminal record.

☐ Decide whether I want this person to also be property guardian for any assets that I leave to my children.

☐ Talk to this person in detail and ask for his or her commitment.

☐ Understand that a judge will make the final determination. Provide specifics about my relationship with this person, the reasons why I have selected him or her, and why the person is the best choice to raise my children.

☐ Put contingencies in my will should the guardian's life situation change.

☐ Nominate one or two backup candidates should my first nominee be unable to serve.

ATTORNEY-IN-FACT FOR ADVANCED DIRECTIVES INCLUDING LIVING WILLS

Estate planning isn't just about who gets what after you are gone. It also addresses the financial and healthcare decisions that can dramatically affect your dignity and quality of life in the event you become unable to make decisions or communicate for yourself while you are still here. Throughout the course of my career, I have frequently seen major family conflicts arise over a seriously ill or dying person's wishes when there was neither a living will nor a durable power of attorney named.

Fortunately, you can easily communicate these choices in advance. The trio of legal documents addressing these matters is typically called advanced directives and usually consists of a living will (which is actually not a will at all, but rather a short document in which you spell out what medical care you do and do not want), a durable healthcare power of attorney, and a durable financial power of attorney. Durable powers of attorney enable you to select someone to represent your interests should the need arise. The person who serves in this capacity is referred to by a number of different titles including attorney-in-fact, agent, proxy, or surrogate. I use the term "agent." Although when acting as your agent the person is required to sign his or her name followed by the phrase "attorney-in-fact," he or she is rarely an attorney at all. Most typically the agent is a family member, loved one, or friend. You specify ahead of time what that person can and cannot do for you in formal documents called durable powers of attorney.

Whereas the will only takes effect upon death, advanced directives are employed when someone is on life-support, mentally incapacitated, or otherwise unable to make decisions about his or her health and finances.

Each state has its own formats for living wills as well as durable healthcare and financial powers of attorney. These documents are relatively simple and inexpensive to prepare. Attorneys often offer a package deal for helping you to create all three at one time. Some states allow you to combine the living will and durable healthcare power of attorney in one document. Many people choose to fill them out without an attorney. If you choose this route, I strongly recommend having an attorney review what you have written. You can find forms and additional information by calling local hospitals, going online at www.aarp. org and www.partnershipforcaring.org, looking in form books, and even visiting doctors' offices. However, keep in mind that you are not limited to the choices outlined on the forms. You can be very specific when you describe what powers the agents have and what medical care you do or don't want to receive.

Durable power of attorney matters can be very confusing. Common questions I am asked on this subject include the following:

For my healthcare decisions, do I need both a living will and a durable healthcare power of attorney?

Ideally, you should have both a living will and a durable healthcare power of attorney (referred to here as "the agent."). These reinforce each other in very positive ways. A living will serves as a written guide to loved ones and doctors, as an important vehicle for communicating your wishes to your agent, and expresses your wishes to other family members and loved ones who might be unaware of your preferences. If you don't feel anyone can serve as your agent, then this document becomes your only chance to express your wishes. However, living wills are not honored in every state and even when they are recognized, someone must produce the document and fight to have it apply to the specific medical situation at hand. Powers of attorney help strengthen the living will because some medical providers, nursing homes, hospitals, and even your loved ones might ignore the living will when they disagree with your wishes. By having an agent there on the spot, especially a feisty and strong agent who knows and respects your wishes, it is much harder for a medical provider to ignore him or her, and thus, you. Additionally, with all the new and developing technologies, it's impossible to anticipate each of them in a living will. Whether or not you have an agent, be sure to communicate your wishes to your doctors and make certain they agree to honor your decisions. Otherwise, consider finding new doctors.

The most challenging part is choosing your agent. After you have an agent and an alternate or two in mind, the document itself is relatively simple to complete. Note: Unlike a financial power of attorney discussed later, be careful about writing highly specific instructions to your agent when drawing up a durable healthcare power of attorney. Some states view these instructions as limits on the agent's power to act. Be very specific in your living will and more general in your durable healthcare power of attorney.

What happens if I don't have a living will and durable power of attorney for healthcare or financial decisions?

If you do not have a living will and have not formally named an agent, should a time come when you can't make and communicate medical or financial decisions for yourself, a judge will pick someone to make them for you in a costly, public, lengthy process of proving your incompetence and determining who your agent should be (often called a conservatorship or guardianship proceeding, similar to appointing a personal representative if you die without a will). The court could easily appoint someone who does not know your wishes, even if he or she is a close family member.

The Supreme Court has given every competent adult the right to consent to or refuse medical treatment. In an emergency, however, if you do not have a designated agent, the hospital protocol or a doctor you may not even know decides what care you get until the court names a guardian for you. Hopefully, the doctor would speak with your immediate family, but there is no guarantee of any discussion or that the doctor or hospital would honor what they say. Do you really want someone to decide your medical fate on the basis of a spiral procedure notebook written under the guidance of malpractice attorneys? Do you want your family to agonize over life-and-death decisions? What if they can't agree or have different philosophies from yours? What if you did not want artificial life support and you end up getting hooked up to a machine for years? What if you wanted to try anything, even something considered experimental, to stay alive but doctors feared your family would sue them and so didn't give you everything that was available?

As for financial decisions, what if loved ones can't wait for lengthy court proceedings? I've often heard stories of desperate loved ones signing checks for the ill person or doing other banking transactions for him or her. Not only is forgery a serious crime, but financial management involves far more than merely signing checks.

Finally, these documents are especially important for unmarried couples. Unmarried partners are generally not considered immediate family members under state law. Without these documents, your partner's input can be severely limited if even allowed into the decision-making process at all.

How detailed can I get in my living will about healthcare choices and other issues?

You are not limited by the choices listed on your state's living will form. You can express your wishes with regard to additional specific medical procedures. That said, here are a few of the issues you will see on most state forms, as well as some of the very important ones that don't always show up. Whether or not these issues are listed on your state's form, please consider each of them and communicate your choices. If you are worried about protecting your assets from a medical or nursing facility or from Medicare, consult with an attorney who is an expert in asset preservation.

Life-sustaining treatment including procedures, medications, and machines that keep you alive but do not cure you if you are terminally ill. Talk over the different options with your doctor to make more informed and perhaps more specific decisions here. Note that you can stop or refuse these treatments and still receive food and pain relief.

Artificial feeding and pain relief.   Be sure to specify when you do or do not want these. For example, you might feel differently about a temporary feeding tube that aids recovery versus a permanent feeding tube in a terminal condition.

Mechanical ventilation (breathing machine).   Consider different situations when this issue might arise. For example, would you choose this treatment if doctors knew you could never breathe on your own again and that you would always require other life support such as artificial feeding?

Blood transfusions and organ transplants.   Certain cultures have strong beliefs about these procedures, yet they do not always show up on state forms. Again, consider the specifics of what is and isn't acceptable to you—for example, blood from family members versus from a blood bank.

Organ donation (anatomical gifts).   As you prepare your living will, start to think about whether or not you want to make anatomical gifts, more commonly called organ donation. While a living will is an excellent place to state your choices about organ donations (yes, no, or different answers for specific organs), there's a need for speed when the time comes. It's best to carry an organ donor card much like you would carry a driver's license or other identity card. If you wish to donate your organs, do both. Explain your decision in your living will, then call your local hospital to obtain a donor card and carry it with you. Why make loved ones guess and face pressure from doctors or each other?

Burial wishes.   As with all the choices involved in this section, discuss these with your loved ones and write down your wishes. Many clients use the living will and health-care power of attorney process to talk about burial wishes, funeral service preferences, and other important matters. Consider writing up a statement about what you want, resources to accomplish these things, and other specific choices. Attach this letter to your will, your living will, and the powers of attorney to make sure your loved ones know your wishes. You'll help them immeasurably by having already made choices they might find difficult to make for you. There's no guarantee loved ones will follow your directions, but the more people who know your wishes and the clearer you are about them, the more likely loved ones will follow them.

What kind of power can I give an agent when I write a durable power of attorney for financial matters?

You can give an agent broad, sweeping powers to manage all financial decisions including investments or you can limit the agent to, for example, day-to-day activities. Other choices or specific powers can include using your assets to pay your expenses and those of your family; buying, selling, and maintaining property or other assets; filing and paying taxes; and managing your retirement accounts, in addition to any other activities you specify.

Be aware that banks and brokers are extremely cautious even if your agent has a signed power of attorney.

During the past two decades banks and brokers have increasingly requested an agent to prove he or she has been given power to act by obtaining a court order. One way around this doubt and delay is to create a living trust, place your assets in it with yourself as trustee, and name your agent as the trustee who will take over when you are unable to serve yourself. If you want an extra guarantee that your selection won't engage in any funny business, you can even name a bank as co-trustee or as successor trustee to the agent you select.

What is the difference between durable and limited power of attorneys?

When choosing a healthcare or financial power of attorney, you choose which specific powers you give, and the words you use—for example, "limited" or "durable"—can make all the difference in the world. You may have encountered a limited power of attorney if you've sold property and let the real estate agent attend the closing for you. However, for medical decisions and financial matters, you'll want to execute "durable" powers of attorney so they stay valid if you were to become incompetent.

Also, you are not limited to or required to give any of the specific powers found in a general form you may have purchased in a form book. State law governs powers of attorney and the actions of agents named in them. Even though each state has different suggested formats, you can still pick which powers you give and define precisely what those powers should be.

When will an agent act for me?

Typically agents can act only when you cannot make decisions for yourself, understand the nature and consequences of the choices at hand, or are unable to communicate your decisions. Some states, however, let you determine under what circumstance you want your agent to take action. In some cases, you can give your agent the power to act as soon as you sign the durable power of attorney.

What are some other things that I should remember?

Your agent will need to have the signed original power of attorney to show doctors, financial institutions such as banks, and so on, in order to act. Give copies of living wills and healthcare powers of attorney to your doctors and copies of all three to your loved ones. Tell others where the original is, but keep it in a safe, easily accessible place where someone can bring it to the hospital in an emergency—or to a bank for financial matters.

You must name an agent when you are competent. It never hurts to get a letter from your doctor at the time you draft a power of attorney or living will that says you are in good mental condition. Once you need an agent, it's too late to name one.

Some states require you to record a power of attorney in a county recorder's office for it to be valid.

Can I change my mind about whom I picked as
my agent?

You can change your mind about whom you want to be your agent by creating a new power of attorney, for either healthcare or financial matters, and gathering up and destroying all the old ones. If your state has required you to file the power of attorney with the county recorder, be sure to record your cancellation of it and record the new one in its place.

MAKING THE CALL

The person you choose to act as an agent on your behalf is an extremely important decision. You need to trust that person completely, and most people select a family member or friend. Although the law requires an agent to act in good faith, in practice there is no real supervision until someone petitions the court to have the agent removed and asks for an accounting, a contentious and costly move.

You should choose someone who has the strength to make difficult decisions according to *your* wishes—and not his or her own or those of others. Medical advances continuously create new choices. It is impossible to anticipate every situation that could happen. Likewise in financial matters, it is impossible to anticipate all scenarios that might require action.

Here is a checklist of some helpful questions to ask yourself when selecting a medical decision-making agent:

☐ How well does the person know me and my philosophies? Does that person share those philosophies?

☐ Is this person capable of understanding my medical condition and proposed medical treatments?

☐ Does this person live nearby? If not, is the person willing to travel and spend time in my hometown while I am in the hospital?

☐ Will this person be strong enough to make the decisions I want, or will the person be too emotionally involved to carry out what I've asked for?

☐ Is this person thorough, persistent, and strong enough to stand up for my wishes with doctors and medical care providers? What about with my family members who may have differing opinions?

When picking a financial agent, ask yourself the following:

☐ Does this person know my wishes and philosophies? Does this person share them?

☐ Does this person have the knowledge, time, and energy to perform the agent's duties?

☐ Can this person do the legwork, phone work, and so on, to fulfill the job?

☐ Will this person be strong enough to make the decisions I would want? Does the person have a conflict of interest as a child or a spouse?

☐ Do I intend to pay the person a fee for his or her services?

A central theme of this book is that you are free and able to make important life choices. By making them, you increase your peace of mind today. I've talked about your stuff, but you are your greatest asset and must serve as the quarterback of the team all the way to the finish line. Now that you have thought about whom you want to help you carry the ball and which of your loved ones you may involve, it's time to consider two other distribution dilemmas you might confront, beginning with issues of fairness.

Recognize That Fair Is Not Always Equal

Equalize, equalize, equalize! It's the battle cry of many legal and estate planning experts who adamantly tell us this: If you don't want to cause your family pain, then treat them all the same. And hoping to keep peace, the vast majority of us blindly follow this cookie-cutter approach when writing our wills. Yet even if you undergo the most painstaking accounting imaginable when dividing up things, your family can still explode after the will is read. Many adult children feel an absolute entitlement to what *they* think is their fair share—and for most, fair means equal. But they each define equal in their own way. On top of that, it's common for them to equate the inheritance with your love.

Perceptions of being treated unfairly tend to create or exacerbate jealousies, sibling rivalries, and other simmering tensions. But unfortunately, in real life, our possessions and assets do not easily reduce to equal fractions. Depending on the people and circumstances you are faced with, there's an entire forest of practical issues that arise in the tug of war between what's equal and what's fair:

- Should you factor in the value of time and attention? For example, should the child who lives near an ailing parent be rewarded for having provided more care? Conversely, should grandchildren who live far away receive something extra for having missed out on cookie baking sessions, outings to the ballpark, and dance recitals that you shared with their cousins who happened to live nearby?

- If your partner has children from a previous marriage, do you leave them an inheritance equal to your own children's?

- Is it fair to leave more to your daughter who chose to be a schoolteacher and still needs the down payment for a house than to a thriving, investment banker son with money to burn? Further, if you paid more for one child's college expenses, should you settle the score in your will even though they all had equal opportunity to go to the school of their choosing?

- Should some of your children receive a greater inheritance to take into account that their college expenses are still ahead of them when older siblings are in the picture who have already completed their educations?

- Is it fair to skip a generation and leave everything to your grandchildren? What if one child has two children and another has four? Is it fair to leave half to your spouse and half to your adult daughter when your spouse needs more to keep up the house you've always shared together?

- Is it fair for parents to spend most everything on their own retirement or bequeath large sums to good causes rather than leave it to their children?

However you decide to answer these questions, what your heirs will see and hear tends to be far more complicated than a "one-for-you and one-for-you" distribution system can ever satisfy. As we attempt to balance out the inheritance equation, most of us will find far more at stake than just the numbers.

The bottom line: There isn't one simple way to divide assets and personal possessions that will work for every family, because each family is unique. That's why the remainder of this chapter is filled with stories describing how others have grappled with tricky fairness issues. Reading their experiences before deciding how to divvy up the bounty can help you identify your own wishes, along with the needs and expectations of your loved ones. Whatever the details of your own story, keep in mind there is no one right or wrong answer—no one knows your family situation better than you do. And in the end, remember this: The failure to make a decision is the least fair decision of all!

GOLDEN RULES OF FAIRNESS

As you read through the following stories, you will find many illustrations of how these Golden Rules play out in real-life scenarios.

1. Equal is much more about sense than about dollars—counting your savings and assets is just the tip of the

iceberg once you start thinking about what equal means to your loved ones.

2. Each family member will have his or her own ideas about what equal and fair are—and you can bet their spouses and in-laws will have equally strong opinions.

3. The choices are yours—and yours alone (within the bounds of the law)—to make.

4. You can't please everybody all the time, so aim for outcomes you think are fair, given your particular circumstances and what you know now. (See sidebar: Aesop's Fable.)

5. Examine your motivations to avoid making inaccurate assumptions or allowing prejudices to skew the great fairness abacus in the sky.

6. Consider your plans through each of your loved one's eyes, especially if you are planning to leave numerically unequal amounts.

7. How heirs will view your last wishes has more to do with the relationships you have with them in the here and now than anything you can say or do in your will.

8. Finally, communicate why and how you reached your decision—whether now or later, in person or by video, in writing and/or in the will itself.

WHEN ONE SON OR DAUGHTER HELPS OUT MORE THAN THE OTHER(S)

"My son and his family have really pitched in over the years to help me, more so than my other children."

One long-held belief is that adult siblings compete with each other for future bequests by helping their aging parents. Research increasingly has proved just the opposite. In

AESOP'S FABLE

When considering equal versus equitable issues, keep in mind this Aesop's fable. It underscores that no matter how hard you try, *you can't please everyone all the time.*

The Man, the Boy, and the Donkey

A Man and his son were going with their Donkey to market. As they walked along, a countryman passed them and said, "You fools, a Donkey is to ride on!"

So the Man put the Boy on the Donkey, and they went on their way. But soon they passed a group of men, one of whom said, "Do you see that lazy youngster letting his father walk while he rides?"

So the Man ordered his Boy off the donkey, and got on it himself. They hadn't gone very far when they passed two women, one of whom said to the other, "Shame on that lazy lout to let his poor little son trudge along."

In response, the Man brought the Boy up with him on the Donkey. By this time they had come to the town, and passers-by jeered at them. The Man asked what they were scoffing at and they replied, "Aren't you ashamed of yourself for overloading that poor Donkey with you and your hulking son?"

The Man and the Boy got off the Donkey and tried to think what to do next. After much deliberation, they decided to cut down a pole, tie the Donkey's feet to it, and raise the animal to their shoulders using it. They walked along like this, hearing laughter from all who saw them. Soon they came to a bridge where the Donkey kicked one of his feet loose, causing the Boy to drop his end of the pole and the Donkey to fall off the bridge into the river where he quickly drowned.

"That will teach you," said an old man who had followed them along their way. "Please all, and you please none."

fact, just as I have seen with my own clients, studies show that the more children there are in a family, the less each one is likely to contribute toward caring for a parent. Often the caretaking role falls on one sibling alone, usually the one who lives closest to the parents. Is it fair to split an estate down the middle when most of the care fell on one child's shoulders? As people live longer, and more baby boomers start parenting their Moms and Dads— often while still raising their own children (the sandwich generation)—families will increasingly grapple with the issues shown in the following story about Miriam.

Miriam was a 75-year-old widow with three children and six grandchildren. For many years she had lived independently until her arthritis limited her ability to easily get around. Four years ago she accepted an offer from her son and moved across town to live in his home with his wife and their three children. Since then, Miriam has contributed to monthly household expenses, kept the house tidy on days when she was feeling up to it, and often cooked dinners for her teen grandchildren when her son and his wife were running late. In the last two years, however, her health has declined even more. A mild heart attack followed by a cancer scare required Miriam's son and daughter-in-law to each take time off from work to care for her, as well as ferry her back and forth to a number of doctors' offices for follow-up appointments.

Miriam also has two daughters, each of whom lives about two hundred miles from her son's home. One is a busy advertising executive, married with two young children. Although she helps Miriam on occasion and religiously sends birthday and Mother's Day gifts, for the most part she and her husband show up only for Thanksgiving or brief periods during the summer when the children are out of school. The other daughter, a single working mom with one daughter, rarely has time off work for visits, but regularly phones Miriam each week to check in.

Although she had always intended to leave her modest estate equally to the three children, Miriam recently started thinking it might be fairer to leave most of it to her son. After all, he and his family have devoted more to her than the other children in terms of time, money, love, and affection—not to mention letting Grandma live with them, which she was well aware wasn't always easy. Further, as Miriam explained to me, "the importance of sticking together through life's ups and downs" was an important value to her. Long ago, she had cared for her own ailing mother, much the same as her son had done for her.

When we discussed her situation, I helped Miriam think of ways to accomplish her desire to do something extra for her son's family without leaving a bitter taste in the mouths of her other offspring and grandchildren. Did she really blame them for not visiting more or helping her out, given the circumstances? The solution we came up with was to leave her son, Jack, as the sole beneficiary of a $20,000 insurance policy (from her days working as a secretary) and to distribute the rest of her cash estate equally to her six grandchildren, which would come out to a few thousand per child. Further, as a goodwill gesture she leveraged her sentimental "small stuff" to head off any hard feelings. She gave her valuable fine English china that she had received on her wedding day to her single working daughter and her collection of seven antique Royal Doulton figurines to her married daughter. She also left several pieces of costume jewelry to each of the grandchildren for them to remember her by. All other possessions—which were of little financial value and had already been incorporated into her son's home upon moving in—Miriam left to Jack.

She then wrote a letter to the children to explain her thinking, saying that there would be a little something in cash for the grandchildren to put toward their educations. Further, while she was proud of and loved all three of her children, she had decided to leave the proceeds of her insurance policy "to Jack, who has sacrificed a lot to take care of me and even missed vacations and work when I was sick. I want him to use this money to take Donna and the children on the vacation of their dreams." She then went on to describe the special meanings of the family heirlooms she was passing on. Within days, both daughters and their children called to thank her and express support for the plan.

Did Miriam do what was fair? Yes, in her mind and for her family. But similar situations will lead to different— though equally effective—outcomes. I've seen children who have stepped up to the caregiving plate, much like Miriam's son, say "thanks, but no thanks" to a parent's offer of compensation using their will as the vehicle. One woman explained that the inequality in her father's bequest might threaten the relationship she had with her sister. In this case, after much discussion, the father decided his daughter was right and instead offered her a gift of $11,000 toward the down payment on a house she was buying. Since this sum did not exceed her father's annual gift exclusion, it was tax free for both of them. This was a way he could demonstrate appreciation while still leaving equal amounts in his will. Indeed, many parents who feel that one child is more deserving of their resources will quietly provide for them now by helping to finance a car or fund a vacation. Showing your appreciation while you are still around is often the best way to equalize.

BLENDED FAMILIES: SHAKING IT OUT

"It doesn't make sense. Their entire lives I've loved them all and done my best to treat them all the same. They have never thought of themselves as half-anything."

Today more and more people are getting married for the second or even a third time. When children from previous marriages are involved, things can quickly get sticky when writing a will. Marriages where both step- and biological children are involved are often a major source of conflict in estate planning.

Marcia and Carl, a couple in their early 50s, were married for nearly 23 years and had four children: two together and two from Marcia's previous marriage in her early 20s. They had recently attended the graduation of their youngest and were now planning a month-long excursion to Asia, just for the two of them. This was the dream trip they had always wanted to take. In the wake of the recent tsunami, however, they had become very nervous about leaving the country without having their affairs in order. Like many couples, every time they started to write their wills, they got stuck on an equal-versus-equitable issue that they didn't know how to resolve. In their case, the dilemma was this: How should they divvy up their estate among all four children, since two of the offspring were likely to receive an inheritance from Marcia's ex-spouse as well?

For discussion purposes, I asked them to envision dividing the value of their estate into half. Then I asked Marcia how she wanted to distribute her portion. She readily replied that she couldn't imagine anything other than splitting it equally among the four children. I then posed the same question to Carl. Although inclined to follow Marcia's lead, he wasn't sure if it was really the fairest solution. After all, Marcia's ex-spouse had been gainfully employed for years and would surely leave some type of inheritance to Carl's two stepchildren. But if Carl distributed his half equally among all four children, wouldn't it lead to hard feelings down the road if two received a double inheritance while the other two had only enough money for a rainy day? Maybe he shouldn't leave his share in equal fourths after all.

After he shared his thoughts with me, I gave Carl the assignment of writing a pretend letter to the four children explaining an unequal inheritance to them. Within hours, he called me saying the exercise was impossible to complete. As he passionately explained, "I finally realized that I really couldn't count on what their dad would do. My stepchildren might not see a dime from his estate. Who knows, maybe it would all go to his current wife. Plus, it doesn't really make any sense to leave them less. I've raised the children side-by-side and done my best to treat them all the same. You know, I've never heard them describe themselves as half-siblings. An unequal inheritance might undo the hard work Marcia and I have done throughout the years for them to feel equally treasured and to hang together as a family unit." He concluded, rather poignantly, "I can't stop treating them the same after I die. What's really important to me is that they never question my love for them all."

Again, it's important to note that this was a highly personal decision shaped by what was most important to Carl and his specific circumstances. The following week, another stepparent I worked with came to an entirely different conclusion. This was a stepmother who had never spent that much time with her husband's two daughters from his first marriage. They were already in high school when she met them and lived primarily with their mother. "I have no problem with my husband leaving them their fair share, but we've never been that close. I don't really view them as my kids. I want my share of the estate to pass on entirely to our son." Being married doesn't require mirror-image wills. And being a stepparent doesn't automatically require you to do what Carl did. But whatever decisions you make, stay in sync with your own values.

PUNISHING SUCCESS

"How could you give me less for doing well?"

All of his life, Jim has gone to great lengths to please his parents. He was a star student in school making honor roll year after year. He excelled in sports, even winning an athletic scholarship for his leadership and skills on the soccer field. He worked through college to make ends meet. Upon graduation, he married his high school sweetheart, a woman whom his parents adore. After his recent promotion to vice president of a local bank, Jim bought a beautiful home in one of the most prestigious areas in the community. Further, he was reveling in the news that he and his wife were expecting their first child.

Despite all these good deeds, Jim's parents, the Heatons, had decided to give him 20 percent of their money and property upon their deaths. The other 80 percent was designated for his sister, Ginger, who was in greater financial need. The Heatons simply felt that Ginger, divorced twice with three kids and often in and out of jobs, would need the support more than Jim ever would. As Mr. Heaton noted, "Jim has made us so proud, and he knows it. But the simple fact is, I won't ever worry about Jim. He's established himself. Ginger, however, is a different story. She's our hard-luck child, so to speak, and I know Jim will understand. He and Ginger are very close, and he has always loved being uncle to her kids."

When the Heatons first announced their intentions in my office, I advised them to talk to Jim first before making any final decisions. Within hours, they called me back, slightly shell-shocked. Their always-composed son had gone ballistic on the phone, screaming in no uncertain terms that their plan was entirely unfair. When Mrs. Heaton tried to explain that Ginger had three kids to feed, not to mention college educations to fund one day, Jim shot back, "Look, I love Ginger, but you're punishing me for doing well, don't you see that? You gave her a house. You paid for two weddings. All of my life, I've done everything you asked me. I can't believe you are even thinking of this, especially with a new grandchild on the way."

The Heatons' perception of family bliss had been shattered. In the end, they decided to split their estate between their son and daughter 50/50. But then they went one step further and set up an educational trust for the grandchildren to ensure that each of them would be able to attend college someday. They appointed Jim as the sole trustee.

Again, this is how one family handled their predicament. In another, the child who has done well said to parents, "Look, I don't need the money. Even though I don't like my sister's choices, I do understand why you want to leave your money to her instead of me. Anyway, what

Shelly and I would really like you to leave us is Mom's pewter collection and Dad's baseball cards." In this case, leaving unequal amounts without input from the son would have meant leaving the relationship between siblings in jeopardy. Whatever you decide, there has to be communication—the sooner in the process the better.

SECOND THOUGHTS: EQUAL OPPORTUNITY VERSUS EQUAL COST

"My daughter feels entitled to more money from her inheritance than her brothers since we spent more on their college educations."

When Helen and Bob Clarkson, an older midwestern couple, drew up their will years ago, they kept it simple. They assigned a guardian for their then minor children, two sons and a daughter, and divided their estate equally among the three. But now, Bob is wondering if an equal division was the right decision. After a few glasses of wine during her last visit home, the daughter privately shared some negative feelings about their will with Bob. The source of her discontent was quite simple: The Clarksons had funded all three of the children's college educations, but their two sons had attended expensive private colleges while the daughter had gone to a far less costly state university. The tuition disparity during the course of four years had worked out to nearly $40,000. Bob, a doting father, who adored his only "little girl," was having pangs of guilt. Maybe she had a point. While they didn't have the assets to make up the disparity now, he was thinking that maybe they should leave their daughter more in their will. Helen, his wife, who could best be described as "no-

nonsense" in her demeanor, thought this was all simply ridiculous. "The children should just accept what we give them and be appreciative of that."

I asked the Clarksons whether, in fact, their daughter had been given the same educational opportunities as their two sons. The answer was yes. While she also was encouraged to apply to a private college, she simply had chosen a state university instead. They had always been careful to offer their daughter the same options as their sons. When it came to education, Helen and Bob had religiously made sacrifices and budgeted throughout the years, so their children could go to the college of their choice.

"Come to think of it," Bob commented, "Helen and I always believed it was up to each child to take opportunities and run with them." I asked Bob, "So, what's different now?" A silence followed on the phone as he realized he had answered his own question. In the end, the couple decided not to change their original plans. Instead, Bob wrote a letter to their daughter—making a copy to leave in a file with the will—explaining their views on the matter and the resulting decision to still leave everything equally to the three children.

The decision of another couple I consulted with to leave two children an equal share of assets also met with an unexpected fairness challenge. In this situation, the older daughter had eloped while still in college and was still happily married 15 years later with two children of her own. The younger sister, however, entered her married life wearing a designer gown with two hundred guests in attendance and a sit-down dinner reception—all paid for by Mom and Dad. The older daughter had harbored resentment for years about the amount of money they spent on her sister's wedding.

When the parents announced an intention to leave them equal shares in their will, the older daughter burst into tears. It didn't take much prodding before she poured out her feelings about not only the wedding but a life-long sense that her parents had given more of everything to the younger sister. First, the parents reminded the daughter that she had been offered the same opportunity of a big wedding but had insisted on eloping, saying that she didn't want to go through the hassle of an elaborate wedding. The parents then pointed out the various things they had done for her and her children throughout the years, perhaps to some extent as a way to balance out the money they had spent on her sister's wedding. At the end of the discussion, the disgruntled daughter agreed that a 50/50 split was fair and admitted that she had probably overreacted.

The advance notice about significant estate planning decisions provided the family with an opportunity to deal with unmet expectations and unresolved feelings now—while the parents were still around to help resolve them.

PLANNING FOR KIDS OF DIFFERENT AGES AND STAGES

"I want to make sure Tom and Anne don't spend half of their inheritance to pay for college."

Often parents provide a greater inheritance to some of their children to take into account additional needs for care and educational expenses that are still ahead of them. For example, the McMillans have four children: Justin (age 14), Beth (age 18), Martin (age 24), and Jennifer (age 30). Justin is in high school and Beth is just about to enter her freshman year in college. The older two children have already completed their college educations. If one or both parents survived, wouldn't they pay for the younger children's college education just as they had already done for the older ones? The McMillans decided that all funds should be initially held in a single trust with the trustee authorized to distribute the amounts necessary to finance an undergraduate college education and to provide living expenses for the two children still in school until the youngest graduates from college or reaches age 24, whichever comes first. At that time, the remaining assets were to be divided equally among all the children. In cases like this, when the youngest child comes of age and completes his or her education, the parents should be sure to update their wills. (See sidebar: The Importance of Updating Your Will . . . And Ten Signs That It's Time to Do It.)

SKIPPING A GENERATION

"I gave my son money to send the grandkids to camp and he spent it on his cars!"

Most people who are writing wills want their grandchildren to end up with something. Often, however, they leave everything to their own offspring, hoping that someday a bit will make its way to the grandchildren. But there's no guarantee the grandchildren will ever see a penny of what is left to their parents. And when there's a legitimate concern about the fiscal habits of those next in line, it might be time to consider passing them over and leaving assets to the next generation.

Such was the case for Howard, a widower with major worries about how two of his three children handled their finances. Howard's daughter had no concept of the value

THE IMPORTANCE OF UPDATING YOUR WILL . . . AND TEN SIGNS THAT IT'S TIME TO DO IT

Even the smallest shifts in your family—from moderate tremors to 7.0 earthquakes—can affect your estate plan and the balance of fair to equal. Review your will annually or when any of the following occur:

- Your financial circumstances substantially change (assets are acquired or sold, property increases or decreases in value, and so on).
- New children, stepchildren, or grandchildren are added to the family.
- Minor children become older (thus having different needs to address), turn 18, or complete a college education.
- You want to add a person or charitable organization as a beneficiary.
- A parent becomes dependent on you.
- Your child or spouse dies or becomes incapacitated.
- You or your child gets married, divorced, remarried, or involved in a domestic partnership.
- You move to a state with different estate laws or existing laws change.
- Someone you've appointed as guardian/trustee/executor dies, becomes unable to perform the role, or your relationship with that person deteriorates.
- You change your mind about previously made estate decisions.

of a dollar and often went on shopping sprees, charging outrageous amounts on her credit cards. She had constant arguments with her husband who, despite his best efforts, was unsuccessful in reigning in her spending habits. Howard's younger son had recently graduated from college and was already asking his dad for advice on setting up a retirement account. No worries there! But his older son was into boats and cars. Whenever he got a bonus or big windfall at work, he would immediately spend most of it on vehicular toys. An incident the summer before had really upset Howard. After sending this son money so that the grandkids (his only ones so far) could attend camp, Howard called the weekend before they were supposed to start to see if they were excited about going. Camp? They hadn't a clue. Howard was infuriated.

To protect his existing and future grandchildren, Howard decided to set up a Generation Skipping Trust or GST (see "Common Trust Vehicles" sidebar under Human Law Four) to give the bulk of his estate to the grandchildren. He considered making his younger son the trustee, but realized that would probably create tension between the siblings. In the end, he named his bank as trustee instead. He knew his children might not be happy with his decision, but after all, they were self-supporting and could take care of themselves without further help from him. He worked hard so that they could each have a college education and wanted to be sure that his grandchildren had one as well. If things were left to their parents, the way it looked now, that might never happen.

When Howard told the children about the trust, the younger son said, "That's great, Dad! Now I won't have to worry about paying for college when I have kids." The other son was outraged, telling them about his plans to buy a Hummer with his anticipated share of the inheritance. Howard's daughter was speechless at first, but finally blurted out, "I might never even have any children.

What then?" Howard was expecting these kinds of re-actions and was prepared to stand his ground—which he did!

WHEN FAIR EQUALS ZERO

"But, Dad, the Internet Only Happens Once!"

Increasingly, parents are questioning the wisdom of leav-ing everything to their adult children. While their numbers still remain relatively low, more and more I hear comments like, "Planning my estate isn't a problem for me at all, Elizabeth. I expect my kids to earn their own way." While this sentiment usually comes from wealthier individuals, I also hear it from those with more modest estates. I recently worked with a 30-year veteran of the police force and his wife, a stay-at-home mother who had raised their six chil-dren. The couple planned to give the entire proceeds of their estate to the local Catholic church. They strongly be-lieved that their faith had gotten them through some very rough times—a value they hoped their children would carry forward in their own lives. Having been told from an early age that they were expected to make it on their own, the couple's children never blinked an eye when they heard about their parents' intentions.

However, if you do plan to leave what you have to people or organizations outside of the family, tell your children as soon as possible and be sure you've helped them develop the skills and tools they will need to make it on their own. (For tips, refer to the sidebar "Raising Children to Be Re-sponsible About Money" in Human Law Two.)

Take for example, Richard, a self-made entrepreneur

with millions in the bank from taking his Internet company public in the mid 1990s. He and his wife intended to bequeath their substantial holdings to a long list of charities. As Richard remarked, "I've already given my kids incredible opportunities. They grew up living in the finest neighborhoods and always attended private schools. The best thing we can give them now is the chance to make something of themselves—and of course, our love." Raised in a dirt-poor farming community, Richard struggled from the age of 14 on to help support his mother and brother after the sudden death of his father. Barely graduating from high school and not even dreaming of attending college, he pulled himself up by the bootstraps. Always good with numbers, he discovered a knack for writing computer code while working for a small accounting business and went on to launch one of the first Internet companies. He felt strongly that his children should make it on their own as he did so they could enjoy the sense of accomplishment and pride that comes from succeeding at something through thick and thin. "Besides," he said, "I didn't bust my back all my life so my kids could sit by the pool the rest of theirs."

Richard also expressed some resentment toward his wife for overindulging the children while they were growing up. Unlike him, she had come from an affluent family and saw no harm in making life easy for them. But clearly, neither parent had prepared the children for what was coming. When Jim and his wife recently revealed their plan to leave everything to charity, the news came as a big surprise and caused major upset. Their daughter, a recent college graduate, exclaimed, "But, Dad, the Internet only happens once!" Their unemployed 30-something son, who had moved back in with his parents, having just been laid off by an Internet company no less, was outraged and shouted, "I'll never be able to afford to live where I grew up." Although the children have been barely speaking to their parents since the announcement, Richard and his wife have steadfastly stuck to their plan. But you can bet if Richard dies first, the children will put all sorts of pressure on their mother to reconsider. In terms of fairness, the moral of this story is simple: Don't raise the children like Park Avenue poodles if you're planning to turn them out into the woods. And if you *have* raised them like poodles, it's never too late to help them develop the skills they need.

Surprise! There's Nothing Left to Leave

Older generations are now living much longer than previous generations, often spending more of their accumulated wealth on not only basic living expenses and long-term care, but also on a more active retirement lifestyle. All of this can quickly eat into an estate and leave children surprised or feeling slighted when very little of substantive value is left to pass on to them. As one 78-year-old widow remarked, "I've had to draw the line—living my life to the fullest means spending my children's inheritance. I never thought it would be this way, but I never expected to live this long either. They are just going to have to come to grips with it." Help your children come to grips with it by giving them advanced warning. It will save a lot of heartache and disappointment in the end.

It's not about being equal, it's about being fair—and the way to be fair is by looking at the big picture. Ask yourself what makes the most sense given your own wishes and the needs of your loved ones. Above all, are your decisions in sync with your values and with what you think is most important in life?

Once you've come to grips with your own family fairness issues, you might also want to consider the implications—and wisdom—of using your will to address unfinished business with a significant loved one.

HUMAN LAW SIX
Unleash the Power of Forgiveness

When a relationship with a son, daughter, or grand-child goes through rocky times, what sometimes runs through people's minds is this: "I'm going to cut you from my will. You'll never see a cent." But before acting on thoughts like these, hold on!

It's dangerously easy to use your will as an emotional weapon by leaving less to those perceived as unworthy: a son not heard from in years, a daughter who leads an un-savory life, or a grandchild who only calls when he needs money. When taken to the extreme, this seemingly unde-serving person might be left out of an inheritance altogether.

And sometimes, despite even the best efforts at reaching across the great divide, the most loving choice—and the way to stay true to your own values—is to limit an inheri-tance or restrict access to what you leave. This chapter tells how to minimize the legal ramifications in such cases (See sidebar: Will Challenges and How to Avoid Them) and to have the least negative impact on your family. But for most situations—and for most people—writing a will provides the motivation needed to mend broken fences and leave the family intact.

WILL CHALLENGES AND
HOW TO AVOID THEM

People have been contesting wills for hundreds of years under a variety of circumstances such as these: The deceased made specific promises in life that the will didn't fulfill. A second spouse gets substantial property. One child (or grandchild) gets more than the others. There are no close relatives. The choice of heirs offended the family. Assets are left to a charity deemed to be unsavory by the family.

If a will is thrown out, property passes as if the estate were intestate—just as if no will existed. Although will contests are a real threat, they happen far less frequently and successfully than in Hollywood movies. Most cases are brought after the will enters probate, which means the court has already found the will to be properly executed. Some attorneys take these cases on a contingency basis, meaning a hefty percentage if they win or nothing if they lose. The estate typically pays hourly fees to its attorney to defend the will. For all those involved, the monetary and emotional costs are high.

A will can be thrown out if one of the following can be proven:

1. **Failure to Follow the Technical Rules When Making a Will.** Your will must be signed to be valid (called the execution of the will), and you must be at least 18 years old at the time of signing. The signed document must be a clean copy with no handwritten changes. The signing must take place in front of two (some states require three) witnesses, who are also at least 18 and do not receive anything under the will.

2. **Incompetence.** If the person making the will is under 18 years of age or determined to be mentally incompetent when signing the will, the will can be thrown out. Most states do not define "incompetent" in the laws. But hundreds of years of court cases have produced a

generally recognized four-part definition. The person must: (1) know he or she is making a will, (2) know the extent and value of his or her property, (3) know who would ordinarily be the beneficiaries of the will, and (4) have the ability to understand who gets what under the will he or she is signing.

3. **Undue Influence.** Although the most common type of case, undue influence is tough to prove. Simple persuasion or empty threats are not enough here. Previous court decisions provide a basic three-part test: (1) Someone must have exerted influence directly connected to the signing of the will. (2) The purpose of the influence must be to gain something from the estate for the influencer or someone he or she favors. (3) The influence must destroy the free will of the person signing the will, such that the resulting will reflects the wishes of the influencer and not the person who signed it.

4. **Fraud.** Using deception, one person tricks a second into writing and signing a will that provides benefits to the first person.

5. **Intended Revocation.** If a will is torn, written upon, mutilated, or otherwise very messy, someone can claim the deceased intended to revoke it.

The best way to avoid someone successfully contesting your will is to prove you knew exactly what you were doing when you created and signed it. Here are additional deterrents to will challenges:

- Consider placing a no-contest clause in your will. Each state has its own finer points to consider, but generally these clauses eliminate any bequest to someone who contests the will if the contest fails.

- Include a small but attractive inheritance for someone you wish to cut out altogether. Whether an object with substan-

tial emotional value or a sum just enough to dissuade someone from taking the risk of losing it, this step also solves a
possible omitted heir contest as discussed below.

- Mention each person who would automatically inherit from
  you if you didn't have a will, whether you leave that person
  anything or not, to avoid an omitted heir contest. The law
  assumes you have unintentionally overlooked children (or
  grandchildren if your son or daughter predeceases you) unless you name them in your will. "Children" refers to both
  bloodline and adopted children, including those born after
  you sign the will. Be certain to state in your will that you wish
  to leave them nothing if that's your decision.

- Obtain a physician's letter saying that you were examined
  shortly before you write your will and found able to think
  clearly. An additional step is to have a psychiatrist examine
  you and give a professional opinion in a written report stating that you were competent and not under duress at the
  time you signed your will.

- If you decide to leave someone less than what he or she
  might have expected, include a short statement expressing
  your intent. For example, "I am leaving you only my signed
  baseball. Other considerations resulted in my decision to
  give you nothing else."

- Set up a living trust for most of your assets. Trusts are not
  easily challenged and demonstrate that your plan was put
  into place when you were well.

- Consider having a professional videographer, not a family
  member or your attorney, tape the signing of your will. Include an interview of you and the witnesses by the attorney
  or another person to portray your understanding of what
  you were doing and your sound mind.

- Write a letter to your beneficiaries and heirs explaining your
  choices.

- Refrain from making nasty comments about others. Wills are public documents. You might reconcile with someone and be unable or forget to change your will.

- Give living testimony in court. A few jurisdictions allow you to make a living probate appearance in front of a court, essentially an interview in which the court establishes the validity of your will before you die.

- Don't make handwritten changes or comments on your will. These can invalidate it. Further, don't change beneficiaries or the amounts people get in a codicil. Make a new will instead. Sign only original wills.

- Be aware that a spouse who outlives you has the right to "elect against the estate" in states without community property laws. This means that if a spouse receives nothing or a very small amount, he or she can "elect" to take the share of your probate estate he or she would have received if you had no will. Jurisdictions vary in the amount of time allowed to file this election, but it's generally around five months. A special form must be used. Spouses can waive this right to elect against the will in a prenuptial agreement.

Five Avenues for Forgiveness

Although we would much rather use our wills to make peace than to make a point, it's sometimes hard to know how to do this, especially when there are unresolved issues with loved ones. Rebuilding trust is a valuable step in the estate planning process, and the following guidelines will show you how to get started:

1. **Be honest about the situation.** There are always two sides to every story. Ask yourself what the conflict is really about for you, then consider it from the vantage point of your loved one. What might be the source of

his or her feelings and actions? People often do hurtful things because of their fears. What underlying concern might this person be trying to express? Own up to anything you've done to contribute to the discord and admit your own mistakes. It's also okay to admit, however, that you are still angry, hurt, or disappointed.

2. **Determine what you can do to make things better.** Start by changing your own attitude. Recognize that your assumptions about the situation and the other person could be outdated or simply wrong. Misunderstandings only grow bigger and more complicated until someone decides to change the dynamics. Acknowledge the good, *any* good, you can find in the person or the situation. Once you start thinking differently, you'll start acting differently as well. And when your own behavior begins to change, the other person's will too.

3. **Involve the other person when possible.** Open the door to discussion by inviting the other person for dinner, to go fishing, or to join you for some other mutually enjoyable activity. If seeing the person face-to-face is not possible or practical, send a card to let him or her know you are thinking about him or her and care. Sometimes simply making this overture causes a positive shift. Before meeting face-to-face, consider writing a letter that the other person will never see. Put down all of your nastiest feelings. When the letter is complete, destroy it. Then sleep on your feelings. The next day, ask yourself if you wrote anything that might help the situation if you communicated it in real life. Some people find that meeting together with a therapist or a neutral third party (preferably not a family member) can help facilitate a resolution.

When the other person won't interact, leave a letter or
video with your will or other estate documents that
communicates your feelings and is waiting for that
person to see whenever he or she is ready.

4. **Forgive yourself.** Yes, in the past you may have made
   some mistakes. But now it's time to forgive yourself.
   Wallowing around in your guilt is unlikely to help the
   situation. It only takes your attention away from finding constructive solutions. As for the present, some
   things are simply out of your control: your loved one
   rebukes your overtures, your daughter won't stop
   gambling, or your grandson has a drinking problem.
   Despite your best efforts to resolve challenging relationship issues, there might be situations when you
   decide to limit what you leave someone or to entirely
   cut that person out of your will. Living in an imperfect
   world requires us to make imperfect trade-offs, often
   touching on the most sensitive areas of our lives.
   When this is the case, forgive yourself.

5. **Make peace with the situation.** When it seems impossible to bring everyone together or find agreement, it's
   time to make peace with the situation. You've tried
   your best, now it's time to accept and move on. Although making peace doesn't mean caving in or
   changing your values—after all, you might still need
   to make unpopular decisions—be aware that sticking
   fast to a position might jeopardize family harmony.

Wills That Punish

When unresolved conflicts with significant loved ones per-
sist, the will becomes a tempting device for having the last

word in the matter. But in most cases, it's a temptation worth resisting. A will that is written to punish is guaranteed to ignite the family's thorniest emotional issues. Some recurring themes I've encountered in punitive wills include the following.

LIMITED ACCESS—OR NONE AT ALL— TO A SON, DAUGHTER, OR GRANDCHILD

When a child marries, sometimes the spouse is viewed as pulling the child away from the parents. The reasons for this range from not liking or trusting a new spouse to parents failing to recognize boundaries as the couple establishes the marriage. Wishing to maintain peace with both sides, the son or daughter becomes caught in the middle. When the next generation enters the picture, the situation can escalate to the point that grandparents' access to their own grandchildren is curtailed or even denied.

One woman pulled me aside at a workshop, telling me she intended to limit her son's inheritance unless he divorced his wife. She was not allowed to see her granddaughter because the daughter-in-law accused her of meddling in their married life. The situation had grown so tense that the woman had no other outlet than to drop cards and little presents in the mail for her granddaughter with the hope that some of them would get through. I knew the woman's daughter-in-law and also heard from her about the situation. She said she was so infuriated with her mother-in-law that recently she had told her husband, "You have to either shoot me or Mom."

NEGLECT—REAL OR IMAGINED

Sometimes an aging parent feels abandoned by children, particularly those who move far away, despite their best attempts to maintain the relationship from afar. A child's absence can seem even more pronounced when other siblings who live nearby are involved in the parent's daily care. Further, as the aging parent becomes less active and has more time to dwell on the perceived slight, feelings of abandonment can fester to the point that a decision is made to cut the child out of the inheritance altogether.

This proved to be the case with Fred, a retired electrician, who had made a modest fortune with some excellent investments. Fred was used to getting a lot of attention, so when his wife died he expected his two daughters, Gloria and Charlene, to fill the void. At first, they each visited their father weekly, alternating so that someone was there to cook him a good dinner at least twice a week.

A year after her mother had died, Charlene met the love of her life, married him, and moved across the country. While she explained it was tough to leave her dad, her new husband had a great job on the West Coast and the decision was out of her hands. Fred was very disappointed and felt completely abandoned by Charlene. Although she would still send cards and check in with him each week by phone, that wasn't enough for Fred. Local daughter Gloria, exhausted and frustrated from bearing the brunt of her father's care, began making critical comments about her sister to both Fred and me, such as, "Well, if Charlene came home more often, she would know about this." Her remarks served to fan the flames of Fred's sense of betrayal. In the months leading up to his death from an unexpected heart attack, Fred had become so angry at

Charlene that he had stopped accepting her phone calls. He had also changed his will, leaving everything to Gloria. Needless to say, Gloria and Charlene haven't spoken a word to each other since—and that was ten years ago!

RELIGIOUS TRADITIONS AND
KEEPING THE FAITH

Interfaith marriages have been rising for decades and nearly thirty million adults—close to a quarter of the U.S. population—now live in mixed-religion households. Often, those who become parents choose one religion over the other for the children, leaving one set of grandparents disappointed.

For most people, religion is accompanied by traditions and rituals that have been embraced throughout a lifetime. Emotional dilemmas abound when they are not passed on to the next generation. Many clients tell me how important it is to them that their grandchildren are raised in the family religion. It greatly concerns them when their children marry someone outside of the faith in which they were raised.

While it's illegal in most states to make an inheritance conditional on practicing a certain religion, sometimes parents will simply minimize what they leave to a child who left the family's faith—never mentioning the reasons why.

Children who don't live up to scripture can also be targets. One of the most common examples is when a child divorces. As one devoutly Catholic 72-year-old grandmother said to me about having cut a daughter out of her will, "I was willing to overlook the first divorce, but not the second. She has no morals." Parents' religious beliefs often are also at odds with an unmarried adult child who chooses to live with a partner, further complicated when grandchildren are born out of wedlock. Similar tensions arise on the basis of religious beliefs when same-sex relationships are involved, such as when parents are invited to celebrate their son's or daughter's same-gender union.

CULTURAL TRADITIONS

Religious preferences can be extended to cultural traditions as well. One familiar example is the tradition of parents selecting a spouse for their son or daughter. Even after immigrating to the United States, some parents insist that these traditions be honored, putting them at odds with their Americanized children. Such was the case of one client, an engineer, who told me he had been disowned by his parents and subsequently cut out of their will because he wanted to choose his own wife on his own timetable. Emigrating from India, his parents had raised their children in the United States. His father had established himself as a highly successful engineer in Detroit. Unlike his siblings, the son absolutely refused to abide by what he believed was an outmoded and ridiculous tradition. He ended up moving two thousand miles away and has yet to marry. He has not seen or spoken to his parents or siblings since, sadly causing a great deal of pain for the entire family.

LIFESTYLE AND DELINQUENT BEHAVIOR

Following close on the heels of religious and cultural traditions is a child's general lifestyle or, in the worst of cases, delinquent behavior. Some parents simply disapprove of how their children live their lives—from how they dress to where they live to the career path they have chosen to how wisely they spend their money. Delinquent behavior, often caused by some sort of addiction from alcohol to gambling, can also exacerbate tensions and cause people to seriously consider using their will as an emotional weapon.

JEALOUSY OF CHILDREN'S OPPORTUNITIES AND SUCCESS

While some might find this hard to believe, it does happen. Parents will find fault with children's behavior and claim they are irresponsible when really the parents are angry about having had to work so hard in their own lives. They resent their children because they think the children have had it too easy and aren't doing enough to make their own way in life. Children who come from working class families and have gone onto college sometimes feel their parents have disowned them on multiple levels. While on the surface the parents seem proud of their children's achievements, they can be at odds with their emotions—essentially they don't like the idea of their kids exceeding them. While rare, in these cases parents can be reluctant to leave their children anything at all.

Forgiveness in Action

Despite the temptation to write a punitive will, there is room for forgiveness in all of us. Most people do indeed want to reconcile damaged relationships. The following two stories illustrate the power of forgiveness in action.

TATTOOED FIDELITY

"I never realized how much my son and I had in common."

Jamie had nine tattoos, and his wife, Susannah, four. Between them, they had seven body piercings, two children, and a mortgage. High school sweethearts who had been happily married for more than a decade, the couple resided in a mixed neighborhood and lived in an old gas station that had been converted into a funky home. Jamie was a carpenter while his wife cared for and home-schooled the children. Appearances aside, they were loving parents who lived a simple life within their means.

Jamie, however, was a huge embarrassment to his father, Paul, who had come to my office to discuss his estate planning. After spending his life building a successful insurance firm, he was leaning toward leaving the control of his assets to his older son, Tom. Paul and his wife, who had died two years earlier, had provided well for their two sons and raised them in a "traditional values" household. He described his son Tom as a "chip off the old block" who had followed in his own footsteps. After earning an MBA, Tom joined his father's insurance firm. Like Paul, he was an avid golfer and tennis player, joining the same country club his father had belonged to for many years.

It was an entirely different story with Jamie. While the two attempted to maintain some semblance of a father–son relationship, Paul said he was embarrassed to introduce Jamie as his son. As Paul put it, "He always tries to provoke me, showing up looking like that, especially at family Thanksgiving dinners at the club. For Pete's sake, just look at how he lives and where he lives! He's wasting everything I broke my back to give him. And why does his wife always wear those wrinkly tent dresses? Could his children just once wear socks? How could I trust him with my money? And when is he going to get a real job?" While Jamie's mom had always softened the tensions between father and son, since her passing, the two could hardly speak. Just that past Thanksgiving, Jamie and his family had been a no-show at dinner.

Given that their relationship was so strained, I suggested to Paul that perhaps I should talk to Jamie to feel him out. With a sigh of relief on his face, Paul wholeheartedly agreed. Despite his strong distaste for Jamie's lifestyle, Paul had been feeling pangs of guilt and a sense of failure as a father at the thought of cutting his son out of the will.

A few days later, Jamie and I spoke. He felt that his father was pretentious, superficial, cold, and attacking. Further, ever since he could remember, his father had always favored Tom, a natural athlete and leader in school. Jamie pointed out that this parental favoritism was rather ironic, given that he was far more responsible than his older brother as an adult.

As Jamie relayed it, Tom was still single—a man about town who carried on his arm some "flavor of the month." Ever the dapper-looking host, he was known for throwing wild parties at his expensive home and for piggybacking off his father's success and good name. Jamie wondered out loud whether his father had even mentioned to me his older brother's DUI the year before, concluding that he probably hadn't, which was indicative of his father's tendency to only find fault with him and never his older brother.

On the other hand, Jamie saw himself as a committed husband and father who worked twelve-hour days to support his family. He always had a knack for building things with his hands and had settled on carpentry as a career. He was quite proud of himself, noting that he had earned a reputation for real craftsmanship and attention to detail. Lately he had been receiving more and more calls for custom work in high-end homes. His hope was that he could bank enough money soon to move his family into a better neighborhood with a better school system. Then his wife would no longer need to homeschool their children and could return to her previous work as a graphic designer.

As for his father's estate, Jamie said he wanted nothing. He had long ago given up on having any meaningful relationship with his father, though it was important to him that his children knew their grandfather just as they had known and loved their grandmother. As we concluded our conversation, I realized that Jamie shared many of the same values as his father: family, honesty, work with meaning, faith, and service to his community. He was much like Paul in his commitment to fulfilling his obligations as a father, husband, and provider.

After I shared Jamie's feelings with Paul the next day, there was a long silence on the other end of the phone. I concluded by saying that it was indeed ironic that Jamie had mentioned nearly the same values that Paul expressed to me earlier. Perhaps Paul was missing something and not seeing things as they really were. To do so, he would need to clean his own lenses and replace some outdated views. I encouraged Paul to call Jamie and continue the conversation we had begun. He said he would think about it.

Months later, Paul returned to me with his sons to go over his final estate plan, which now included them both. Paul had decided to leave his business to Tom and his home to Jamie. The balance of the estate was to be equally distributed between the two brothers.

On the path to forgiveness, sometimes all it takes to begin the healing process is to look at things through cleaner lenses.

ROLLING THE DICE

"Whoever would have guessed that our daughter would turn her life around?"

Nothing brings estate planning into clearer focus than a brush with death. And that was the case with the Avery family. A few months earlier, Mrs. Avery, the family matriarch, had suffered a debilitating stroke out of the blue. Since then, she and her husband had started to communicate in earnest about what was going to happen if she ended up "going first." A key issue was what was going to happen to one of their children, 32-year-old Lisa, who had a gambling addiction. It was a messy situation that the family had never come to terms with. Mrs. Avery was worried that when she was gone, the daughter would suffer even more because Mr. Avery wanted to completely cut off his daughter. The Averys had already been to one attorney and still couldn't see eye to eye on what to do with Lisa. They came to me, hoping to get unstuck.

Of their four children, Lisa had always worried them the most. Growing up, she perpetually seemed to fall in with the wrong crowd. Unlike her siblings, she wasn't interested in her studies or sports, and the Averys considered it nothing short of a miracle that they had managed to get her through high school and college. For a moment in time, they thought Lisa had finally "found her way" when she landed her first job straight out of college as a sales rep for a sporting goods company. Within months, however, she had mysteriously been laid off. She claimed that the company was downsizing, but the Averys suspected that something else was going on. While she had managed to get other sales jobs, she was forever short on money. Mrs. Avery always came to her rescue, covering her cash short-falls on everything from rent and utilities to car payments and clothing. As an exasperated Mrs. Avery said, directing her glare at her husband, "When your daughter calls and tells you her heat has been cut off and it's the dead of winter in Connecticut, what are you going to say? Make a fire?"

Finally last year, the Averys' other children told them the root of Lisa's problem. Apparently, their daughter was addicted to gambling to the point that she would cut short her workdays or miss work altogether to go to New York City for offtrack betting. They had pleaded with Lisa to seek professional help, but she refused to acknowledge the problem. I suggested that instead of addressing her problems in their will, they show some tough love now. A threat of no inheritance might motivate her to address the problem in earnest. Given Mr. Avery's attitude of being "finished" with her and Mrs. Avery's fragile health, we concluded that I would phone Lisa to discuss the situation.

Just like her parents had warned, Lisa was completely defiant and even incredulous on the phone. Our conversation lasted just long enough for me to convey that because of her problem, the Averys were seriously considering cutting her out of their will. Days later, I got a call back from Lisa. This time she admitted that she might have a "slight" problem and that she had tried to get help but just couldn't stop gambling. As her guard came down, Lisa admitted "off the record" that since her mom has been sick, she's been worried about not only losing a loved one, but also the source of her financial bailouts. With Mr. Avery in the driver's seat, she knew she'd get nothing.

I suggested to the Averys that they drive to Connecticut to meet with Lisa in person. They did, and soon after Lisa began a treatment program. After she completed the program and returned to work, the Averys set up in their will a protective trust for Lisa with an initial five-year term. At the end of that time, if she were still gainfully employed and self-supporting—as well as meeting other criteria of being financially stable—Lisa would receive the remaining proceeds of her trust.

About a year later Mrs. Avery suffered a devastating second stroke. Lisa asked for a job transfer to be closer to home. She was then able to help care for her mother, who passed away shortly after. Today Lisa continues to be a successfully recovering addict and has reestablished a warm, loving relationship with her father.

On the path to forgiveness, sometimes all it takes to turn things around is a wake-up call.

Scattered Bullets

When we fall short in the forgiveness department and continue to take aim with our will, the bullets scatter and hit the people standing nearby. Siblings, grandchildren, and other family members can easily get damaged in the line of fire. You not only pass on an inheritance but unresolved conflicts as well. Cutting a loved one out of your will can affect not only your immediate family but the generations beyond.

TROUBLE ON THE OTHER SIDE

"My parents left my brother out of their will. Now he badgers the rest of us for handouts and is threatening to take us to court."

"Suddenly we started getting Christmas cards, birthday gifts for nieces and nephews, and even flowers for no reason one day!" said Yvonne, shaking her head, who was giving me a haircut. Yvonne was telling me the story of her delinquent brother who had been left out of her mother's will when she died. Initially Yvonne's brother went to great lengths to rekindle relations, in hopes that Yvonne and her two sisters would part with some of their inheritance. Only now it was no longer a laughing matter. Recently, her brother had become increasingly aggressive, constantly badgering them with phone calls night and day to ask for help, from paying his rent to bailing him out of jail after being charged with resisting arrest in yet another drug-induced stupor. Now, he was threatening to file suit against his mother's estate to claim what he felt was rightfully his. The sisters were worried. Each of them had already planned to use the inheritance to help fund their children's college educations. What would they do without it? And, what about court costs? To say the least, dealing with their brother was causing significant stress in their lives.

Yvonne's situation isn't unique. In my line of work, I often hear similar stories of payback time when children are left out of wills. Unable to direct their anger at the parents, the person who was cut out from the inheritance takes out his or her hostility on siblings, ranging from persistent calls for handouts to threatening court action. Parents, thinking they have done the right thing—but never discussing their will with their offspring before dying—inadvertently pass the problem on to the other children to deal with.

In Yvonne's case, the proceeds from her mother's estate were relatively modest, valued in cash at approximately $110,000, to be distributed equally among her three daughters. If the case went forward, the sisters were told they could easily face $10,000–$15,000 in legal fees.

Yvonne's mother had made a common mistake when eliminating one child's share of her estate. She had failed to leave a small, but attractive inheritance—whether an object with emotional value or a "just enough" cash sum—along with a no-contest clause in her will. These clauses generally eliminate the original bequest to someone who unsuccessfully contests the will. (See previous sidebar: Will Challenges and How to Avoid Them.) In this case, had she left her son $10,000 and included a no-contest clause, he probably would have accepted it and gone off on a binge. And that would be that. At a minimum, she would have saved her daughters a lot of nail-biting stress and heartache.

SHORTFALL COUSINS

"My brother and his kids were left nothing, and I feel guilty."

Siblings are not the only recipients of scattered bullets, often grandchildren are as well. Consider the case of the Heckmans. They had two sons, one of whom they hadn't seen or heard from in many years due to a misunderstanding. Last they knew he had moved to Florida—and that was seven years ago. The other son lived in the Heckmans' same town with his wife and three children. When drawing up their wills, the Heckmans felt they had no choice but to bequeath everything to the local son and his family.

Fast forward eight years later. The Heckmans have since died, first Mrs. Heckman and then her husband, leaving their nearby son as sole heir to a modest estate. Within months of Mr. Heckman's death, the renegade son suddenly reappeared in town with a charming wife and two children in tow. He made contact with his brother, who was thrilled to hear from him, and they quickly reestablished their relationship. The two families started to share dinners together and weekends at a cabin that had been in the family since the brothers were boys. Soon, however, Mr. Renegade's children started to ask questions like, "Who were Grandma and Grandpa? Why did they give everything to our cousins and nothing to us?" Even Mr. Renegade's wife started to grow perturbed after eyeing yet another beautiful ring on her sister-in-law's finger, originating from the senior Heckmans' estate. She couldn't help but share this frustration with her children. "You're being punished for your father's mistakes," she exclaimed.

Then one day Mr. Renegade asked his brother for a set of keys to the cabin so that he and his family could come and go as they pleased. The request was initially met with a mumbled "let me think about it" by the brother, who was starting to think that what he had actually inherited from his parents was one big mess! On one hand, he thought it was entirely fair to allow unrestricted access to the cabin. On the other, didn't his parents leave it to him and to him alone? After days of agonizing over how to respond, he finally hit on a wise solution. He offered Mr. Renegade a key under the following plan: Both families could enjoy unrestricted access to the cabin, but would begin to split 50/50 the cost of all repairs, improvements, and taxes. In exchange for sharing expenses, he offered to deed half the property to Mr. Renegade with the stipulation that the cabin would ultimately pass on in equal shares to their five children. The offer was enthusiastically accepted, and the two families have continued to grow even closer ever since.

Initially, the only thing these brothers shared from their parents' estate was the big mess. But thankfully, they found a way to avoid passing *that* on to the next generation.

Leveraging Legacy Vehicles

In the preceding stories, using a legacy vehicle such as a letter or video to explain one's actions might have greatly minimized after-the-fact conflicts. Those who have been unable to make peace with a family member, or people who have set up protective trusts, often find it incredibly freeing to express themselves through legacy vehicles. As one woman told me, "Writing down my feelings meant I could finally let go of them." Here are two examples.

THIS IS THE BEST GIFT WE COULD GIVE

Dear Tim and Susan,

I love you dearly, as did your mother. We always said that having you two made our lives complete. We would talk about you often, remembering the old days with the four of us around the card table for Friday night fish sticks and how when we would all go camping, you two would complain about carrying your own backpacks. Well look at you now! I'm so proud of the responsible adults you've become.

Like us, you both put your families first and nothing could make me more proud. I know it's not always easy. Tim, I know you put your dream of starting your own shop on hold when the babies came faster than you and Maria had planned. Susan, how you manage alone with the girls is beyond me. Working, getting your real estate license, and raising the girls leaves you no time for yourself. As you know, your mom and I saved every penny for years to buy the house. You've both told me how much you'd each like to have your own homes (or even mine) someday. I know you two love each other but don't always see eye to eye. We all know your spouses and boyfriends have also had ideas about what is right for you. Life can sure get complicated!

Your mom's medical bills ate up most of what we'd saved, and now all I have left is this house. When your kids were born, your mom and I saw how much you loved each of them. We decided then and there that this house must go to give our grandchildren what each of us went without or broke our backs for—a college education. Victor Gomez, our attorney, will explain the details, but rest assured that each of your children has a nice chunk of change to make it easier for them to earn a degree. I love you both and hope you see this as the best gift we could give. That's my greatest hope.

Dad

YOUR LIFE IS ABOUT YOU

Dear Kim,

I love you with all my heart and think of you every day—how we'd chase waves at the ocean, go exploring for shells when we'd visit Grandma, your beautiful smile, and your dreams for your life. This letter is very hard for me to write. I haven't seen you since the last time you came over to the house drunk. Of course I want to help you, but you have to help yourself first. I finally came to realize that my loans only made it easier for you to drink. I don't want you to booze away what little I have to leave you. So I've decided to set aside something to help you keep a roof over your head, a clean and safe place for you to live. Roger McCarthy at Metropolis and County Bank is the trustee, and I've instructed him to pay your rent each month directly to the landlord or rehab facility.

Your brothers Tom and Bill can't get money for you, so don't bother asking them. And if you ever fight my will, you don't get anything at all. My greatest wish is that you become sober and make those dreams you had real. You've said all I ever do is criticize and say you were never good enough. I don't see it that way, but I am truly sorry for anything I have ever done to hurt you. I hope that one day you might understand that my only intentions have been to love you and help you become a responsible adult. I've relived your childhood every day and punished myself more than anyone else could for every mean word I said.

Now that I'm gone, perhaps you might see that your life is about you—that you have so many gifts to

*give this world and yourself. I've instructed Roger that
should you get sober, stay sober, and hold a steady job
for three years, you'll receive half of the money to
manage for yourself. Whatever you don't use, if there
is any left, will go to your nephews. Do it, my darling
daughter. Get healthy, even if just to spite me.*

I love you now and always,
Mom

If you can, make peace with your loved ones while you
are still here to enjoy it—and know that your family will
be thanking you long after you are gone. At the very least,
make peace with yourself. Whatever you do, don't take
shortcuts in the forgiveness department.

*Once you've made choices about what to leave and
how to leave it, it's time to get everyone on the same page.
Have you found ways to let your loved ones know why
you made those choices? If not, you are setting them up
for grief gridlock!*

It's Not What You Say, It's How You Say It . . . *and if You Bother to Say It at All*

If you take one thing away from this book and from reading the stories that are scattered throughout it, I hope it's this: Wills, like most everything else in life, are ultimately about people—in this case your family and loved ones. And when it comes to successfully dealing with people, it's all about communication. First with yourself and then with those around you—a spouse or partner if you have one, your circle of loved ones, and the team members you select to help you.

When we talk about communicating it's not just about the possessions you are leaving, but also about yourself—your values, hopes, dreams, and ultimately your legacy. Because communication is so critical to giving your family peace, both while you are still here and after you are gone, this final chapter is dedicated to addressing key communication issues such as: How much should you share with your family about the details of your estate? Why is it important to communicate before and after you make any decisions? How do you start conversations and get loved ones involved? What are some troubleshooting techniques you can employ along the way? How can you engage your own parents in conversations about their wills and estate plans? I'll address these questions and more in this chapter along with sharing tools and techniques that have helped my clients create goodwill in their own families throughout the estate planning process.

How Much Should I Share?

If you can make it work for you and your loved ones, tell them everything there is to tell, leaving no surprises for after you are gone. Time and time again I have seen that when family members feel they have been well informed and given a chance to provide input, they are far more accepting and less apt to create chaos. However, as with everything else when taking the Good Will approach, consider your own family circumstances when deciding how many details to reveal. In some cases less is more.

Communicating your plan is a gift in itself. Even when you prefer not to disclose exact figures or specific decisions, at least give loved ones a sense of what might be coming—or not coming—so they can adjust their lives accordingly. It's also important for them to know that you have taken care of things and that they won't be stuck sorting out your affairs. Often expectations and anxiety about estate-related matters fester silently for years, subtly—and sometimes not so subtly—affecting the relationships of everyone involved. By communicating your intentions when you are still around, issues that are simmering below the surface can be uncovered while there is still time to address them. My clients often report dramatic improvements in their here-and-now relationships with loved ones simply by bringing these issues to light.

If you are planning to leave someone far less than he or she expects, an unequal inheritance, or nothing at all, it's still better to put everything out on the table up front. Hearing it straight from you—ideally during a calm moment—dramatically reduces the likelihood that family members will contest your wishes, bicker, or backstab later down the road. After a death when loved ones are grieving and not always rational, the opportunity for misunderstanding increases exponentially. If they've already heard about your plan directly from you—or at least the gist of it—there will be less confusion and misinterpretation. While holding discussions doesn't guarantee that people will embrace your wishes, dialogue can take you a long way toward gaining acceptance. The more forthcoming you are, the sooner your loved ones can be able to work through any differences or disappointments—all while you are here to listen or even change your mind.

However, despite all of the benefits of full disclosure, in some cases it doesn't make sense and can even be harmful to loved ones. For example, young children are not emotionally mature enough to handle such discussions. Or with older offspring who are to receive a substantial sum, you might not want to share your entire balance sheet with them for fear the news will unmotivate them, especially if they weren't raised with a strong work ethic or sense of responsibility. In such cases, it might be best to leave a letter or video explaining your decisions to be given to them after you are gone or when they are mature enough to digest the information. If your family relationships are already strained and sharing everything could create more acri-

mony, waiting to reveal the contents of your will until after you depart might be the best choice. Only you and
your spouse or partner, if you have one, can make that
call. You know your own family best.

In all circumstances make sure to let people know that
you have taken care of your will. At the very least make
certain that team members know what is necessary for
them to do their job, such as where to locate the necessary
documents. Of course, never withhold critical information
concerning advanced healthcare or financial directives. For
example, if you have executed a living will—an expression
of your wishes concerning life support and treatment in
the event of a terminal illness—copies should be provided
immediately to all family members who might be involved
with your care.

*No matter how much you can or cannot tell loved ones
now, there isn't anything that you should not tell them
after you are gone.* At the very least, everyone should
know the rationale behind your decisions so if there are
any disappointments among heirs they can direct them at
you rather than each other. Remember, whatever they
imagine will be far worse than the truth. People are always
better knowing what you were really thinking, rather than
making guesswork out of your intentions.

In addition, make sure that you have adequately addressed the distribution of your "small stuff"—your household contents and personal belongings with significant
sentimental and/or financial value. As previously discussed
in this book, one of the first things that occurs after you go
is the division of personal property. The smoother the distribution process the better, and the smoother everything
else will go during this very emotional time when your
family needs to feel secure.

Equally important, don't overlook the enormous power

of legacy vehicles referred to throughout this book. In addition to expressing the thinking behind your estate plan, legacy vehicles communicate life lessons, milestones, hopes and dreams for the future, blessings, and even regrets or apologies. These vehicles enable you to leave behind the gift of who you are and what's most important to you in life. They are often remembered and valued by your loved ones far more than the personal possessions or money you leave them. Even simple "I love you" letters can be enormously comforting, particularly for younger children, and impart a lasting sense of goodwill. Although constructive and detailed discussions with your loved ones ahead of time are invaluable, it's always a good idea to also put everything down in writing or on a video. Once you are gone, family members will have their own memories of what was said during your life. Human nature predicts that they will each believe that their account of what happened is the right one. Leaving your own version is the best way to prevent after-the-fact disagreements among your heirs.

If during the course of time your plan changes substantially and you have already disclosed its contents to family members, make sure to share any major alterations and reset expectations as necessary. Ill feelings will most likely erupt among your children—or between them and their spouses—if they are banking on the Taj Mahal and end up with far less.

Overcoming an Uneasy Silence

Are your children sneaking around your house looking for your will? Don't be surprised if they are. I frequently hear stories like this:

While watering her parents' plants during their trip to Florida, Carla did a roof-to-basement search for estate documents. The suspense was killing her. She had always felt uneasy raising the topic of wills with her aging parents. Recently, though, her sister-in-law Kathleen had mentioned to Carla at a Fourth of July picnic, "Your mother gave me the sweetest gifts—her silver candlesticks and the wicker porch furniture. Isn't she a doll?" Carla's blood boiled. Kathleen was already planning where "her" new furniture would go, while Carla was now dying to see if she and her husband were going to be rewarded for all the extra help they had given her parents throughout the years.

When it comes to wills, most people don't want to think—much less talk—about their own death, while their children themselves grapple with how best to broach the subject. And even when parents do raise the issue, they often find themselves dismissed with comments like, "Oh, Mom and Dad, that won't happen for a long time!" or "What are you talking about? You're going to live until you're 100!" Nobody likes to think about this stuff. Wills tug on our most primal fears: security, separation from loved ones, and the unknown. Even in the most open and loving families, there can be an uneasy silence when the conversation turns to death and money. People fear upsetting what is a workable status quo. They build walls around certain topics—chief among them, money—to avoid rocking the boat. Others just don't want to figure out their finances much less face the prospect of giving Uncle Sam another dime. For many who are working on their wills, the chief stumbling block is simply the stress of reflecting on their own lives. The process forces an examination of not only one's finances, but of relationships as well.

What if you see something that you don't like in yourself or in your family? And who among us has no regrets?

As simple as it may sound, the key to overcoming these roadblocks is communication—the sooner the better. At the very least, creating the Good Will is an opportunity to set things right, build bridges, or close gaps—ultimately allowing your last wishes and last words to become a positive force within the family. Opening up discussion not only helps you complete the process, but also frees your family from any hidden tensions they might be carrying around. Before moving forward, take a good long look at where you and your loved ones are now. Here are some tools for doing just that.

Guidelines for Getting Together

What's the best way to bring the family together for estate discussions? Start by thinking about how you communicate with your loved ones about everything else. Then use these same methods for estate discussions. It doesn't have to be fancy or complicated.

For example, if you primarily communicate with your children through e-mail or snail mail, send a letter to everyone telling them that you are thinking about your estate plan and would like their feedback. If you typically call them, pick up the phone or schedule a conference call with the principal players. If your family gets together a few times each year in person—be it for the Fourth of July, Thanksgiving, or a family camping trip—talk to them about your will on one of those occasions. If they all live nearby, consider informally discussing it over breakfast, lunch, or dinner. If you prefer not to mix business with family gatherings, especially if there are touchy issues that would upset people on a festive occasion, organize a special family business meeting.

Of course, long before holding a special meeting, you've been keeping your eyes and ears open to family dynamics and have been passively gathering data along the way, as discussed in Human Law Two. In the earlier stages you probably weren't directly discussing money or estate issues at all, rather just reflecting, observing, listening— essentially taking the pulse of your family. What brings them joy? What concerns them? What are their strengths and weaknesses? How healthy are their relationships with each other, their spouses, their own children, and other relatives—as well as with you and your spouse or partner, if you have one? By sleuthing, you probably were able to pinpoint some hot buttons, take steps to head off potential problems, and start to build bridges along the way.

For most people, it becomes time at some point to openly share plans with loved ones. Use the following suggestions to ease the process and facilitate discussion.

DON'T BLINDSIDE

Whatever method or combination of methods you choose for discussion, try not to blindside your heirs. Before discussing the estate plan, consider sending a letter ahead of time outlining some of your key thoughts, such as:

Dear Everyone,
*   Here are some of the main things we are thinking*
of putting in our will. We want to give you the
opportunity to think about them before we all get
together to talk about this next Thursday at dinner. If

*you have any questions, feel free to call us ahead of
time or just bring them on Thursday.*

> *Love,*
> *Mom and Dad*

Giving others time to process and think about what you
are going to be presenting can go a long way toward head-
ing off confrontation. While some people are fast proces-
sors, others might need time to think about things. Going
too fast can lead to misunderstandings. Based on their expectations, some family members might have a negative
emotional reaction when they read for the first time what
you have in mind for them. After reflection and rereading,
however, they may cool down and become more level-
headed. A letter of forewarning also allows anyone with
an issue he or she would be uncomfortable raising in front
of everyone else to speak to you alone beforehand. A little
advance notice can go a long way toward peacekeeping
and productive discussions later.

Further, some people may not be on speaking terms. A
letter or phone call about your estate plan will generally be
well received. However, if you haven't had contact about
anything else lately, don't renew the relationship by con-
tacting them about money. Reconnect about something
else first before bringing up your estate right off the bat.

GREASE THE WHEELS

For some families a little treat or bribe from you and your
spouse for the entire group can motivate everyone to finally address the issues surrounding your will and estate
plan. While some parents can afford to treat the family to
a ski vacation in Aspen, a simple dinner out will work for

most. And when you have everyone gathered together, don't forget to enjoy quality family time. It's easy when you are in the process of planning, updating, and fretting over your estate plan to let money discussions dominate everything and take over your interactions with loved ones. Use time together to reinforce that your family is about a lot more than possessions or money.

AFFIRMATION

Address loved ones on a human level first. Start the discussion with an affirmation: Tell each individual or your group of heirs how much they mean to you and how you love them.

RESTATE THE IMPORTANCE OF TALKING ABOUT YOUR ESTATE PLANNING

Explain to everyone why this topic is important to you and them. Be clear that the goal is to create the best possible plan so that the family can flourish in your absence. Start off by giving an example from this book of an estate that was improperly handled because family members failed to communicate.

TREAT THE DISCUSSION AS A DOOR OPENER

Don't come across as "this is written in stone." Rather, position the discussion as an opportunity to get their feedback to help you make better decisions. Encourage family members to express their opinions regarding priorities, values, goals, and advisors. While ultimately the final decisions will be yours, explain that you will be taking their input into account.

CREATE A COMFORTABLE ENVIRONMENT

Make sure that you and your loved ones have adequate time to talk together. Don't scrunch a discussion into a quick phone call or tack it on to the end of a long meal. Pick a convenient time and place (if you are getting together in person) for everyone.

IF NEEDED, SET SOME GROUND RULES

Before you begin, consider laying ground rules for what is and isn't acceptable in the conversation. Establishing an environment of mutual respect is invaluable, especially where relations are strained. For example, "Sometimes we have problems getting along, and people have brought up painful things from the past. For today's discussion, I want to draw a line in the sand to prevent this from happening. No one can talk about any hurt that happened before breakfast this morning!" Other common ground rules are no interrupting and no raised voices. Let everyone know that if rules are violated, there will be some sort of consequence for the offending party, such as having to take everyone else out to dinner or not being able to talk for fifteen minutes. Be creative, but let your family know that you are serious about keeping the discussion constructive. (See sidebar: Blooper Patrol.)

CALL A TIME-OUT

If two or more people become deadlocked on a subject, take a five-minute break. Be it by phone or face-to-face, when members return to the meeting have them say something they appreciate about the person next to them or by birth order if talking on the phone.

DON'T DO ALL THE TALKING

As important as it is to get your thoughts across, it's equally important to listen and acknowledge the concerns of others. If you encounter an emotional outburst, take the time to acknowledge hurt feelings. When family members feel understood and acknowledged, compromise may be easier to come by. While it's true that some loved ones may not know what is best—be too young, irresponsible, addicted, and so on—inviting and hearing their input will help them "buy in" to the final result.

LISTEN TO THE SILENCE

Sometimes silent or nonverbal communication makes the loudest noise, if only you are listening. When people are dealing with sensitive subjects or talking about things they are anxious about, their body language provides valuable cues about what they are thinking and feeling. Is one family member sitting on the edge of the room, away from everyone else? Does your son always cross his arms on his chest when he's feeling defensive? What does it mean when your daughter won't look you in the eyes when she's saying something? Listen to their vocal tone and be aware of your own. Does your voice become gruff when you are trying to make a point? Are you speaking more forcefully than usual in an attempt to get things settled quickly? Is your husband anxiously breathing through his mouth in a fight-or-flight pattern, making everyone else around the table feel more nervous and tense? If you pay attention to how people are acting—and not just their words—you'll gain a wealth of information.

Talking to Your Parents

By now, after reading this book, you're probably wondering if you'll inherit a set of conflicts when your own parents pass on. Adult children may hesitate to mention estate planning to their folks because they don't want to upset them with thoughts of growing old and dying. Worse yet, children don't want to appear as "money grubbers" or as trying to take over their parents' affairs prematurely.

How do you initiate a discussion without causing misunderstanding? The bottom line is that you need your parents to give you an outline of what they want to have done and who they want to do it. The key is to seize natural opportunities in everyday life. Here are a few conversation starters. For simplicity I have directed them at parents, but they could easily be applied to grandparents as well as other beloved relatives or intimate friends who are getting older. These starters can also be modified and used to initiate discussion with siblings about an inheritance they will someday be sharing with you.

"I'M PLANNING MY WILL"

Use your own will as a launching pad for discussion. For example, you could say, "I've started planning my will and wonder if you have any advice for me. I bet you guys might have some from your own experience." And you might add, "By the way, I don't want to pry, but is there anything I should know about how you've set things up with your own estate?"

BLOOPER PATROL

Oops, so now you've done it. You've just launched a communication blooper. Or maybe you're the bloopee who has just been hit hard by a zinger, intentional or not. What is heard depends on not only what was said, but also who said it and the listener's own biases. So what can you do about invisible zingers flying around the table when the family gathers? I'll give you some suggestions in just a bit. But first, here are a few examples of how bloopers unfold.

Blooper One: Grief or Greed?

Sherry and Marco were in Ohio for the funeral of his mother, Justine. Sherry and Justine had a close and loving relationship. In her grief, Sherry was looking for something tangible to hold onto from this woman who had meant so much to her. Sherry's first thought was something that Justine had promised to give her one day—a string of pearls that her husband had given her on the day Marco was born.

After the funeral service and a quick dinner, Sherry and Marco were getting ready to go to the airport. When Sherry was helping in the kitchen, she shared the story of Justine and the pearls with Marco's sisters and asked if she might take them with her. Pans dropped as they gave her an icy stare.

WHAT SHERRY SAID: Justine always promised me the pearls Marco's dad gave her when Marco was born. Do you think I could take them back with me so I'll have something of hers to cherish?

WHAT SHERRY MEANT: I loved Justine so much. I'm devastated and want a little piece of her to hold onto and keep close. The three of you are such good women and I bet Justine wanted you to have the rest of her jewelry, but she always promised me the pearls. I would love to start wearing them now to feel her close to me. Can you help me through this tough time by letting me take them home with me?

WHAT THE SISTERS HEARD (AND THOUGHT): We just got done burying Mom, and Sherry is already asking for some loot. She's not really even one of us anyway. How dare she!

Blooper Two: Just Who Does She Think She Is?

Early one morning Elaine answered the phone and heard that her younger sister had been killed in an auto accident. Elaine lived three thousand miles away from the rest of the family. Although devastated, she was trying to keep it together enough to get to the airport for the next flight out west. As she was packing, her first cousin Cora called, crying uncontrollably, wailing how life was so unfair and how awful Elaine must be feeling. Although cousins, Elaine and Cora had spent little time together growing up and hardly knew each other. Elaine couldn't get a word in edgewise. When Elaine finally cut in to explain that she had to get to the airport and that she'd see her soon, Cora wailed, "What's wrong with you? Why aren't you crying? Didn't you love her?" Elaine couldn't believe her ears.

WHAT CORA SAID: What's wrong with you? Why aren't you crying? Didn't you love her?

WHAT CORA MEANT: It's hard to know. Following a tragedy, people sometimes say insensitive or thoughtless things. In cases like this, it's healthier not to think too hard about what happened and just let the comment zing on by.

WHAT ELAINE HEARD (AND THOUGHT): This blood relative who hardly knows me is screaming at me about how I should show my grief as if she owns my sister's death. It's almost as if she's rejoicing in the drama. I'm out here alone and can hardly move, nevertheless get to the airport in 30 minutes. How dare she judge me and my love for my sister? Just who does she think she is? Knowing her, she's probably already told my family how cold I was, positioning herself closer to my ailing father to get some cash in his will. Why did she even bother to call? This is all so unreal.

Blooper Three: Disrespect or Admiration?

After much thought, Chris and Samantha decided to name their son Jeff as executor of their wills if they were to die at the same time. They chose their daughter Karen as their healthcare agent if they were unable to be that for each other. They invited Jeff and Karen out to lunch to go over their plans. Chris explained to them that they had elected Jeff, if willing, to serve as executor because they knew Karen was busy with her small children. Karen hit the roof. "Dad, you sure haven't changed. You've never respected my brain. And now, yet again you pick *him* over me." An oops moment all around.

WHAT CHRIS SAID: We'd like Jeff to serve as executor. You're busy with small children.

WHAT CHRIS MEANT: Jeff is in an office every day. His wife can take care of the kids in case he has to work on all the estate paperwork at night. Parenting is the toughest and most important job on earth. Karen is a great mom, especially given that she's on her own. We don't want to burden her with all the filings and the time it would take to be executor. Asking her to be my successor healthcare agent is a huge statement of faith in her. Karen has so much on the ball—she's a good problem solver, too. It would mean a lot to me to have her serve in such an important role.

WHAT KAREN HEARD: You're a girl and not very good with numbers. We never liked your ex-husband and told you so. Now you're just a single mom who doesn't know squat about business. We respect your brother more than you—that's why we didn't pick you.

Even with the best of intentions, misunderstandings or insensitive remarks about death, wills, and estate plans are inevitable. Add a little anger, resentment, or meanness and the zingers can really sting. It's easy to find yourself on either side of a blooper. When you do, try the following:

1. Take a deep breath in and a deep breath out. All of us have strong emotions about money, death, and family.
2. Ask yourself what was said, what was meant, and what was heard or thought.

3. Recognize that you can choose what to do next. Although you can't change what happened, you can decide what to say (if anything) as well as when and how to say it—in person, by phone, or in writing.

4. When—and if—you choose to speak about the blooper, first affirm your love for the other person involved. Then remind that person that this is an emotional time for everyone.

5. If you are on the sending end of the blooper, apologize. Admit that what you said might not have come out the way you wanted it to. Tell the person that you recognize it may have been misinterpreted. Then share what you really meant. Ask the person how you can move beyond this together to a better place.

6. If you are on the receiving end of the blooper, explain what you heard and ask the other person what he or she really meant. Sometimes people just don't think before they talk. Other times, they think too much and say things you would rather not hear them go on about. If you don't get the explanation you are looking for, find a way to make peace with the situation for yourself—either by letting it be water under the bridge or by viewing the experience as a valuable lesson in what to expect from that person in the future and what you can do differently next time.

7. When discussing a blooper with the other person, avoid "I always/never" and "You always/never" statements. Don't get caught in the "I said/You said" or the name-calling game. Instead try this, "When you said _____, I heard _____ , and felt _____." Be sure to listen to what the other person says back and let the person finish his or her thoughts before responding.

8. Finally, remember that we are all human! Sometimes we're the blooper, sometimes we're the bloopee, and sometimes we're right in the middle of a communication tornado. Keep your cool as best you can until you can address the situation with less emotional charge.

PERSONAL STORY

Another way to jump-start the discussion is to relate in a by-the-way fashion the unfortunate story of a neighbor or friend who failed to discuss estate issues with their loved ones. Here is a simple story that two brothers, Alex and Josh, told their parents as a springboard for opening up communication:

ALEX: I see that Mr. Orloff's house is for sale.

JOSH: I thought he wanted one of his kids to get it.

ALEX: Well, I hear that he never made a will. Now all his stuff is tied up in the courts, his kids are squabbling, and no one will get the house.

JOSH : Mom and Dad, you know Alex and I love you. We have our own lives now and have both been working hard. We know we aren't the Rockefellers, but we've been wondering what decisions you've made about your own house. We don't want to end up like the Orloff kids! How can we help you take care of things so this doesn't happen to us?

USE THE NEWS

From Terry Schiavo to 9/11 to Karen Ann Quinlan, national and global news can be used as a springboard for meaningful discussions with parents about their wills and last wishes. You can also share articles with your parents from magazines or newspapers that describe will conflicts or disasters resulting from unclear communication. Follow up by asking, "What would you have done or what would you have wanted us kids to do in that situation?"

WHAT IF?

Often asking "what if" type questions works well. For example, as your parents depart on a trip, you could say, "I don't want to sound morbid, but you never know what might happen. What if something did? Are your wills in place, and is there anything that you want to share with me?" Explain that you just want to be sure their wishes are followed and to know what to do in the event of an unexpected emergency. Or, you could simply ask, "Mom, have you given any thought to what will happen with all your stuff if you actually sell the house and move into that retirement community you keep talking about?"

JUST SAY IT

In a family with open and honest relationships, direct communication often works best. The woman we mentioned previously whose parents downsized, leaving many of their household contents to another sibling, just flat out said to her mother, "I know you love us all, but it simply drives me crazy to see my sister get everything just because she lives closer to you and Dad!" During this woman's next visit to her parents' home, her mother walked her around the house and asked which things were most meaningful to her. The next year when the parents came to visit on a road trip, they brought to her home as many of those items as they could fit in their car.

There are many ways—both direct and indirect—to help your parents open up about their estate plans. It may take several conversations before you make headway. On the other hand, your parents may be just as eager to start the discussion as you and your siblings are—but they too might be grappling with where and how to begin. Concerned that the discussion might rattle their children, they may be waiting for *you* to initiate the conversation.

Taking The Good Will Approach

As you set out on the Good Will adventure, remember that the lynchpin of this approach is communication. And as an approach—rather than a step-by-step progression—you'll find that the seven laws presented in this book shed light on the full range of *human* issues that arise during estate planning for both you and your loved ones. By addressing these human aspects—and not just the legal and financial ones—you'll be better prepared to leave a legacy of both values and valuables. The following ten communication guidelines will help you create goodwill in your own life and the lives of those you care about the most:

1. Check-in with yourself to identify what you really want and what values are most important to you.
2. Talk to your spouse or partner and get on the same page.
3. Communicate your legacy, not just who gets your stuff.
4. Consider your family's needs and expectations before making decisions.
5. Consult with professional advisors.
6. Tell your loved ones what you put in your will and other estate documents.
7. Make sure people know who does what (executor, trustee, and so on), not just who gets what.

8. Let someone know where everything is located (the will itself, important documents regarding finances, and so on).

9. Express your last wishes in your own words—in person, through writing, and/or on video.

10. Share your love!

AFTERWORD
It's Up to You . . .

Dear Reader and Friend,

I salute you! By this point, if you are still with me, it's clear you have people in your life you love dearly. I'm certain you will want to make the most of whatever you have to give them.

Beyond doing just that for my own loved ones, my personal legacy has become helping others develop theirs. For many years the work of guiding families as they create the Good Will—building their relationships and estate plans on stone—has brought me great joy. Yet as you heard at the beginning of this book, after people around me learn what I do they always share tales about wills gone wrong in their own families. So many stories! So much unnecessary grief! I finally realized it was time to find a way to communicate the Good Will approach to a wider audience than I could ever reach one client at a time.

I only wish I had written this book sooner. Then I could have given it to my own father. Or to the teary-eyed woman sitting next to me on the flight to Chicago that I'm on now as I write this to you. She just explained to me how five years ago her mother's will tore the family apart, causing painful divisions that remain to this day.

I've never forgotten my father's words to me from two decades ago, "It's up to you kid. Pass it on." This book makes it possible for me to do just that.

We are all in this world together, and now it's my turn to ask you to pass it on. Celebrate your own life's legacy by sharing with family and friends your insights from reading this book, your personal stories, and—most of all—your love. Remember that in the end, you are the greatest gift you have to give.

It's never too late or too early to start.

Wishing much goodwill to you and your loved ones,

Elizabeth Arnold

We would love to hear more about the successes and struggles you encounter while developing your will or estate plan and how you are able to use the tools presented in this book.

For details on submitting your stories and for updated information on Creating The Good Will, please visit the author's website www.creatingthegoodwill.com

FOR YOUR NEXT EVENT OR GATHERING . . .
CREATE GOODWILL!
Elizabeth Arnold is available as a speaker and workshop facilitator on Creating The Good Will and other customized estate planning topics for:

- Conference Groups
- Professional Training
- Spas and Retreats
- Forums and Corporate Board Meetings
- Private Gatherings
- And More . . .

For details on these services and private family consulting in estate planning, visit www.creatingthegoodwill.com, e-mail Elizabeth@sowingseeds.com, or call Sowing Seeds at 415-359-9090.

INDEX